AF622013

STATUS OF SINGLE WOMEN IN INDIA

JOINT WOMEN'S PROGRAMME PUBLICATIONS

	Rs.
Status of Rural Women in India	75.00
Status of Nurses in India	60.00
Status of Women in Quran (Urdu)	05.00
Good News for Women (Bible Study) (English, Tamil, Kannada, Telegu, Bengali and Hindi)	05.00
Women in Organised Movements	45.00
Women in Praise and Struggle (Bible Study)	05.00
Vision and Service (Bible Study) (English and Hindi)	10.00
Women and Law	05.00
The Problem of Dowry in Bangalore City	05.00
The Devadasi Problem (English and Kannada)	05.00
Indian Women in Media	12.00
Changes in Christian Personal Laws	03.50
Child Labour in Bangalore City	30.00
The Women's Decade 1975-85, An Assessment	30.00
The Basavi Cult	05.00
Women in the CNI Diocese of Delhi	05.00
Pavement Dwellers in Calcutta	15.00

Status of Women Series

STATUS OF SINGLE WOMEN IN INDIA

(A study of spinsters, widows and divorcees)

N.S. KRISHNAKUMARI

Joint Women's Programme Publication

UPPAL PUBLISHING HOUSE
NEW DELHI-10002.

UPPAL PUBLISHING HOUSE
3, Ansari Road, Daryaganj, New Delhi-110002

For

William Carey Study & Research Centre
14/2 Sudder St., Calcutta-700016
and
Joint Women's Programme

© William Carey Study and Research Centre
1987

ISBN 81-85024-22-7

PRINTED IN INDIA
Published by B.S. Uppal, Uppal Publishing House,
New Delhl-110002 and printed at New Era Printers,
B-223, Naraina Indl. Area, Phase-1,
New Delhi-110028.

FOREWORD

The single woman today is asserting her right as an individual in all walks of life. However, in the Indian context her status is an area of discrimination. This discrimination cuts across all sections of women.

In the Indian society where a woman's existence is only that of an appendage to a man, whether she a daughter, a wife or a mother, any deviation from this pattern is considered unclean, evil or diseased. A single woman therefore has to wage a losing battle against the existing social norms and prejudices. In the Joint Women's Programme we have been very concerned about their problems whether they are single by choice or circumstance. Of course the former condition is a very small minority.

Single women in our study fall into three categories :

1. Spinsters—those who have not married.
2. Widows—those who have lost their husbands.
3. Divorced women—those whose husbands have left them.
   All three categories suffer the same discriminations and are looked down upon for not having fulfilled their important mission in life, that of being married and dying while the husband was alive.

The discrimination differs in degree in the various religious communities but the general social stigma attached to them prevails.

We hope the study which was so essential for us in our effort to understand women in the Indian society will also be of help to others, who are concerned about the women's question.

JYOTSNA CHATTERJI
Associate Director
Joint Women's Programme

ACKNOWLEDGEMENTS

I wish to acknowledge my sincere thanks to Mrs. Jyotsna Chatterji, Associate Director, Joint Women's Programme who inspired me to start this study on single women. Though I must confess that I had a desire to study the problems and plight of Hindu widowed women, it was her inspiration which kindled my desire to examine the problems of spinsters, divorced and separated women as well.

My sincere thanks are due to Dr. Shantha Mohan who patiently went through the report and offered me the privilege of her rich and valuable experience by making necessary additions in the report, and to Dr. Mrs Malathi Somaiah, Indian Institute of Management, for helping me during the various stages of the study.

I also wish to thank Ms. Bina Krishnaswamy for helping in collecting field data and Ms. G. Geetha for both data collection and tabulation.

Through this column I also wish to thank all the institutions who have helped me directly or indirectly to meet single women and the innumerable respondents who co-operated with me and contributed to this study.

N.S. Krishnakumari

LIST OF TABLES

Divorced or Separated Women

All Single Women

CONTENTS

1

The Status and Position of Women

A General Historical Perspective

"The role, status and position of women has been far from static, ranging from what is thought to have been a position of considerable authority and freedom to one of equally considerable subservience."[1]

In vedic society a woman occupied a high position in society. She had equal rights with men and enjoyed freedom in choosing her life partner. Women went to the *gurukula* to receive education and married only after acquiring education. A woman was her husband's equal partner and performed all religious ceremonies along with him. In the joint family her authority was accepted and she had full liberty of action.

Thus according to A.S. Altaker, "Women played a more active economic role and participated in rituals" and "girls in higher society were allowed to undergo the Upanayana rite."[2]

During the post vedic age the position of women slowly began to deteriorate. Altaker sees the period 500 A.D. to 1800 A.D. as one of progressive deterioration in the position of women in society.

1. Jain, Devaki (Ed)—*Indian Women* 'Looking back in history' Romila Thapur published by Director, Publications division, Ministry of Information and Broadcasting, Government of India, Patiala House, New Delhi, 1975 (No. 6 pp).
2. Altaker, A.S.—*Position of women in Hindu civilization from prehistoric times to the present day*, Delhi Mothilal Banarsidas 1973.

With the coming of Manu's Code in the post vedic age the vedic custom of husband and wife jointly taking part in religious functions slowly came to be rejected. Women's rights depended entirely on her husband and he declared that she was not man's equal in her own right. He said that "Though destitute of virtue, pleasure seeking, devoid of good qualities, yet a husband must be worshipped by a faithful wife as God." He further said, "A married woman must not do anything according to her own pleasure, even in her dwelling place. When young she depends on her father, married on her husband, and when old on her son."[3]

During this period child marriage became a common practice and women's education was neglected. Thus women were classed in the same category as sudras.

During the Buddhist period the status of women was slightly better, but from the 8th century onwards with foreign invasions the status of women again began to fall.

Marriage developed into a strict institution where women's individuality was completely controlled by the whims and fancies of her man.[4]

The middle ages were the darkest period for India as a whole, especially for women. With the invasion of Turks and Persians the position of women further deteriorated. During the Muslim reign due to historical necessity women lost all her freedom and ceased to be considered as an important and useful member of society. She was considered unfit for performance of religious duties and was pushed into purdah, due to fear of sexual exploitation. This not only restricted her physical movement but also affected her participation in socio-economic activities. Polygamy set in and with child marriage and lack of opportunity for education, women lost all their identity and personality.

In fact when the British began to rule India the position and status of women was at about the lowest level it had ever reached in the history of the sub-continent.[5]

3. *Ibid.*
4. Gupta, Padmidi Sen—*The Story of Women of India*, India Book House, New Delhi 1974 pp. 84.
5. *Ibid.*

During the British rule efforts of enlightened social reformers to emancipate women resulted in passing various social legislations. Sati was abolished and the age of marriage was raised and facilities were provided for women to acquire education.

Status and Position of Single Women—A Historical Perspective

Having examined the status of women in general during the pre-independence era let us now examine the position and status of single women from vedic times. In order to have a common understanding of who the single women are a definition of single women is deemed essential. Single women are those who:

(i) have reached a marriageable age and are yet not married
(ii) are widows
(iii) are divorced or separated.

These single women, in the absence of male protection and security, are resented by society and therefore lack social status.

Inspite of the fact that widows and divorcees have been married, the fact remains that at present they are single and face certain problems.

Position of Single Women

An analysis of the position and status of single women during the vedic times reveals that they enjoyed a high status. The birth of a girl was not regarded as inauspicious, and marriage was not regarded as compulsory. A girl in vedic India waited until she could find the right partner for marriage, failing which she could even decide to remain unmarried. Further, she had a high sense of security due to her right to paternal property. Child marriages were unknown and divorcees were permitted to remarry. Widows were also allowed to remarry if they so wished, and they were neither disfigured nor prevented from wearing jewels. According to Satapatha IV (1.5.9.) "May these women suffer not the pangs of widowhood. Let these women without shedding any tears and without sorrow first proceed to the house wearing valuable ornaments."[6] Thus we see that single women enjoyed considerable status and authority during vedic times. She was not discriminated against nor was her status lowered because she was single.

During the post vedic age the position of single women slowly began to decline. As marriage came to be considered as a goal for women, the chastity of single women was doubted and hence she came to be looked down upon.

According to Manu the father is responsible if he does not give his daughter in marriage at the proper time, and it was believed that a woman who was not married would be denied admission into heaven.

But it must be noted that even Manu insisted on a worthy husband for a girl. Every man should give his daughter in marriage to an excellent and handsome youth of the same caste, but it is better that a damsel who is marriageable should stay at home until her death rather than the father give her in marriage to a worthless bridegroom. Thus though marriage was regarded as essential, the life and liberty of the girl was considered equally important. She was not disposed off to an unworthy youth like a chattel. Thus the parents of the girl were given a certain amount of freedom to keep their unmarried daughters at home.

However, the parents wanting to relieve themselves of the responsibility and anxious to secure a worthy husband for their daughters as early as possible forced them to marry even before puberty. Thus the custom of child marriage became prevalent. This was done mainly to protect women. The evil custom of child marriage restricted opportunities for mental and physical development of the girls and also accounted for the high incidence of child widows.

Marriage being the only consideration for the parents they offered dowry in order to secure husbands for their daughters. Women whose parents failed to meet the required dowry

6. Quoted from Satapatha IV 1.5.9 Gupta, Padmini Sen—*The Story of women of India*, India Book House New Delhi 1974 pp. No. 57.

demands were harassed, beaten or burnt alive, and those who could not afford to pay dowry at all were forced to remain unmarried. Either way girls were therefore looked down upon by members of their own family as they caused heavy responsibility and expense, to such an extent that the birth of a female child was not welcome in the family. Thus unmarried women were severely condemned and had no place in society.

The position of widows was deplorable. Widows were looked down upon and were not allowed to remarry because "Woman once given away by her parents could not be again given". It was regarded as inauspicious for a woman to be a widow: for her sins somehow seemed to have caused her husband's death. A proverbial high caste, young widow is described as one "who is drudge of all work, in her father-in-law's house, whose bread is sorrow and drink is tears".[7]

Many widows were forced to commit sati and even young virgin widows were sacrificed on the funeral pyre of their husbands.

This evil custom of sati showed that a woman's life was regarded as a burden and not allowed any freedom. She was despised and socially boycotted if she failed to commit sati.

Fear of sexual exploitation by the other male members of the family or society made her lead a life of misery. She was disfigured and made physically unattractive, kept in isolation and forced to observe a certain strict code of conduct.

She was considered inauspicious and was prevented from participating in social and religious rituals. While a widower was encouraged to remarry after the death of his wife, a lot of disabilities were imposed on women who were widowed.

Divorce or separation from the husband was unheard of. Thus early Hinduism held that the marriage union was indissoluble. The later Dharmasastra literature while liberally permitting the husband to remarry during the life-time of the first wife refuses the remedy of divorce to the wife even when completely forsaken by the husband. However, a careful examination of the earlier Dharmasastra reveals that divorce

7. Mehta, Sushila—*Revolution and status of women in India,* Metropolitan Books Ltd. 1982. pp 130.

was permitted before the beginning of the Christian era under certain well defined circumstances. Manu observes that a wife is not to blame if she abandons a husband who is impotent, insane or suffering from an incurable or contagious disease. Abandonment practically amounted to divorce for Manu permits such a wife to remarry if her previous marriage was not consummated."[8]

The couples whose temperaments were incompatible lived separately, while the women kept the benefits of the married state. She kept the marriage open because of the children. She could avoid the unhappiness of living in a state of constant friction with her husband. Legal divorce being unknown this temporary separation provided a sort of compromise between divorce and irrevocable separation and prevented women from suffering social stigma.

However, the problems faced by such women living alone caused married women even though they were unhappy in marriage to continue in the same state. This was further accentuated by their own economic dependence and fear of social boycott.

With the advent of the British rule several social-legal changes began to take place. Raja Ram Mohan Roy campaigned against sati and sati was abolished by law. The widow remarriage Act of 1856 permitted widows to remarry and divorcees were also permitted to remarry under certain conditions. Child-marriage was condemned and slowly women found avenues for aquiring education and employment.

Yet the position and status of women did not change much partly because of the reluctance on the part of women to reform themselves and partly due to society itself which perpetuated their low status particularly that of single women who were doubly exploited.

Post Independence Era

With the advent of Independence the right to equality of status,

8. Banerji, Kanika—*Women and Law* 'Banhi' Joint Women's Programme Publication year 1981 pp No. 24.

equal opportunity in education and public employment was conferred on women. Article 14, 15 and 16 ensure equality before law, prohibit discrimination and guarantee equality of opportunity to all citizens in matters relating to religion, employment or appointment to any office. It prohibits discrimination on the grounds of religion, race, caste and sex. The directive principles of the Constitution also guarantee equality to women, the right to divorce, the right to remarry and the right to property.

Inspite of all this legal freedom guaranteed in the Constitution and the law, the position of women even after 38 years of independence has not changed much. Women continue to suffer indignities and are treated like second class citizens and are subjected to humiliation and ill-treatment in society and this is specially true of single women.

(i) Contemporary Problems

While women are constantly being victimised and exploited by society, single women are victims of a double exploitation by virtue of their being single. They lack the protection of a man and sometimes of a family and therefore are vulnerable to exploitation—economic, social, psychological and sexual.

With industrialisation and urbanisation the socio-economic parameters of the Indian society have changed rapidly. This has lead to the break up of the joint family which was a sort of insurance against all calamities. The single women who once had a sort of social security in such families are now exposed to economic distress, social and sexual exploitation.

Economically they find it very difficult to make both ends meet single handedly. The problem of bringing up children and of providing for their education and marriage becomes the primary goal of most of their lives. Due to the late entry into the labour market some of them find it extremely difficult to manage. Besides, discrimination is also meted out against them in terms of selection, work conditions and facilities. This is specially true of divorced women.

If living alone spinsters and divorcees usually find it difficult to find living accommodation as the landlords prefer married women with children. Socially they face a lot of problems and are not accorded a place in society. Psychologically they feel insecure and experience various mental conflicts and the agony of living a life of utter loneliness.

The position of single women who are economically dependent is worse. Without a job to maintain themselves financially these women are harassed by their own family members and relatives. This constant feeling of dependence often makes them miserable.

In a society dominated by men, single women find it extremely difficult to live. Socially victimised and psychologically depressed, single women play the dual role of both men and women and in the process face a lot of problems.

(ii) Need for the Study

Under such circumstances the need for the study is obvious. A country known for its rich traditions and vast spiritual and cultural heritage where women are worshipped as 'Sakti' also subjects its women especially 'single' ones to such inhuman treatment.

Rapid industrialisation and urbanisation has brought about wide-spread education and employment opportunities and social change in the mental makeup of its populace. Women have begun to think in terms of liberation. Yet the position of single women has not changed. This remains a matter of great concern and therefore their plight and problems need greater attention.

A brief survey of the Census of India 1971-81 shows that numerically they also form a significant percentage of the population and therefore should not be overlooked.

(iii) Census of India (Single women composition)

The following table deals with the distribution of population of India by Marital Status. (1971)

TABLE 1.1

Percentage distribution of population of India by Marital Status. 1971

Marital Status	*Year 1971*	*Total* M	*Total* F	*Rural* M	*Rural* F	*Urban* M	*Urban* F
Never Married	Age group 0—70 yrs	54.90	45.61	54.30	44.81	57.21	49.02
	35 yrs and above	—	3.98	—	3.46	—	6.36
Married		41.82	45.08	42.18	45.70	40.46	42.43
Widowed		2.94	8.86	3.19	9.03	1.97	8.15
Divorced/ Separated		0.25	0.39	0.28	0.41	0.13	0.30

In the above table it is seen that never married females in the age group of 0-70 years account for 45.6% of the population of whom a majority are in urban areas, 49.02 (Rural comprising of 44.80).

The percentage of spinsters as defined by this study, i.e. above 35 years, accounts for a significant percentage of the population. An estimate of the population of spinsters above 35 years reveals that they account for 3.98% of the total female population. A rural-urban distribution reveals that their proportion in urban areas is almost double that of rural areas. Thus urban/rural percentage of spinsters is 6.36% and 3.46% respectively. Under such circumstances the need for a study of spinsters in an urban setting becomes all the more important.

The table of those single due to the demise of the spouse reveals that for the total population the number of widows is more (8.86%) as compared to widowers (2.94%). In contrast to spinsters, the percentage of widows is more in rural areas than in urban areas. (Rural area 9.03%, Urban 8.15%). However, the percentage difference is only of the order of 00.88.

The number of Divorced/Separated females for the total population is 0.39% as compared to 9.25% for males. Surprisingly the number of divorced/separated females in the population is more in rural areas than in urban areas (Female 0.41%) rural, 0.30% urban), inspite of the difference being negligible it is also expected that the proportion of divorced females will be more in urban than rural areas; this being due to the legal avenues available to them.

In general from the above it may be concluded that the proportion of single women in the population as defined by this study accounts for nearly 13.23% of the total population.

Further a study of the distribution of the population of India by Marital Status according to 1981 also reveals a high proportion of single women composition.[1] This is shown in Table 1.2.

TABLE 1.2

Percentage distribution of population of India by Marital Status. 1981 Census

Marital Status	*Total*		*Rural*		*Urban*	
	Male	*Female*	*Male*	*Female*	*Male*	*Female*
Never Married 0-70 yrs.	55.28	45.70	54.74	44.80	56.92	48.72
Married	42.03	45.80	42.25	46.49	41.35	43.46
Widowed	2.43	8.06	2.71	8.23	1.56	7.46
Divorced/ Separated	0.23	0.42	0.26	0.45	0.12	0.32

1. P. Padmanabhan—*Census of India 1981* Series I India Report and table based on 5% Sampler data 1981. Registrar general and census commissioner for India.

The data for the census 1981 is based on 5% sub sample of the 20% area sample. According to this, unmarried females (0-70 yrs) account for 45.70% of the population of whom again a majority of them are in urban areas (48.72%). (Rural 44.80%)

The percentage of widows in the total population is 8.06 as compared to only 2.43 for widowers. Again the percentage of widows in rural areas is far more than in urban areas (Rural 8.23, Urban 7.46). Again among men also the percentage of widowers is higher in rural areas 2.71 than in urban areas 1.56. This is because in a rural setting a widower may not be able to remarry as easily as in urban areas. Wheareas men usually remarry after the death of their wife, widow remarriage is frowned upon.

The number of divorced/separated females of the total population is 0.42% as compared to males 0.23%. But it is surprising to note that the number of divorced/separated is more in rural areas among both male and females (Rural 0.26% Male and Urban 0.12% Male. Rural 0.45% Female and Rural 0.32% Female).

An age-wise distribution of never married females above 35 years was not available in 1981 Census, therefore an estimation of the population of the spinsters was not possible.

The Table 1.2 shows that there are more widows than widowers as chances of remarriage are fewer for women than men due to socio-religious reasons. Again a woman divorcee finds it more difficult to remarry than a male divorcee.

Thus it is observed that the Census of India makes only a statistical reference to their number. Emphasis is not given to their problems. These single women who are an inevitable part of the social system inspite of their significant number in the composition of the population are subjected to many problems.

The problems faced by these categories of women should no longer be neglected or looked at in isolation. In contemporary society where tremendous change is taking place and women are provided with socio-economic opportunities and legal protection, it becomes necessary that they be studied for a careful understanding and insight into their problems.

Further the JWP being devoted to the cause of women's concerns also felt that such a study should be made.

(iv) Objectives of the Study

The following is the outline of the objectives of the study :

1. To find out the socio-economic background of single women.
2. To study the causes for being single.
3. To study the socio-economic, emotional and psychological problems faced by single women.
4. To study the problem single women face in family relationships and social interaction.
5. To study the attitude of society towards single women as perceived by themselves.
6. The suggest measures within the present socio-cultural frame work in order to improve the condition of single women.

2

Methodology

This chapter deals with the scope and methodology adopted for the study. At the outset, the various key terms used in the course of the study have been defined. This is followed by a description of the universe, sampling techniques followed, tools developed for collecting information, method of data collection, statistical techniques used and finally the difficulties faced by the researcher during the course of the study.

(i) Definitions of the Key Terms Used

For the purpose of clarity and proper understanding of the findings some of the concepts adopted in the study have been operationally defined. Single women are defined as those women who are spinsters, widows and divorced or separated.

1. **Spinsters** are those women who have reached the age of 35 years and above and are still unmarried even though they might have plans to marry. Their unmarried status and the upper age limit of 35 years are the main criteria for being considered as spinsters.

2. **Widows** are those women whose husbands have died, irrespective of their age at widowhood.

3 (i) **Divorced** are those women who are divorced from their husbands either legally or by custom or religion. Their separation is irrevocable.

3 (ii) **Separated** are those women who have separated from their husbands, either legally or by custom or religion. Their separation gives scope for reconciliation. Though widows and

divorcees/separated women were married at some time in their life, the fact remains that at present they are single. This justifies the reason for classifying them as single women.

Social problems of single women are classified in terms of the social stigma attached to them, the social restrictions imposed on them and the social boycott or rejection society metes out to them resulting in their low social status.

Economic problems. While for non-working respondents the main problem is that of their economic insecurity and dependence on family members or relatives to meet their basic needs, for the working respondents it is of inadequate income, discriminative facilities and exploitation at the work-place and home.

Psychological problems. The antagonism single women suffer at the hands of society results in several psychological problems they face, such as emotional insecurity, loneliness, inferiority complex, etc.

Having defined the concepts used in the study the methodology adopted for the study is discussed.

(ii) Universe and Sample Selections

All the spinsters, widows, divorced/separated women both working and non-working living in Bangalore city form the Universe for the study. To arrive at an estimate of their proportion the 1971 Census reports were used due to non-availability of 1981 Census data.

At the outset the total female population above 15 years and their number in the labour force was collected for Bangalore city. (Though according to the Sarada Act the minimum age for marriage for females is 18 years it is not uncommon for Indian women to be married below this age). An estimated proportion of female workers to total female population is 11% in the 1971 Census.

The single women population was arrived at by summing the number of unmarried women of 35 years and above and the widowed and divorced/separated groups of all ages. Thus the estimated single women population in Bangalore city was 67,114. To arrive at an estimate of the employed single women population it was assumed that 11% of the single women would also be employed.[1]

TABLE 2.1

(Bangalore) Total Female Population, Women in the Labour Force and the Single Women Population (Working and non-working)

Census 1971	*Total Population*	*Total workers*	*Total non-workers*
Women over 15 years	5,20,980	56,736 (11%)	4,64,244 (89%)
(Single Women)	67,114	7,382 (11%) (Estimated)	59,732 (89%) (Estimated)

The above table gives the total female and single women population and their proportion in the labour force. It was decided to study a 5% sample of the total single women. Since the main objective of the study was to compare and contrast the problems of working with non-working single women it was decided that an equal number of respondents should be interviewed from all the 3 categories of single women.

[1]Absence of any data base on the subject matter of the study necessitated such an assumption.

TABLE 2.2

The distribution of working and non-working respondents by sample drawn and interviewed

Type of Single women	*Working*		*Non-working*		*Total*	
	Sample Drawn	*Sample inter-viewed*	*Sample Drawn*	*Sample inter-viewed*	*Sample Drawn*	*Sample inter-viewed*
Unmarried	62	62	62	23	124	85
Widows	62	62	62	62	124	124
Divorced/ Separated	62	62	62	62	124	124
				Total	372	333

Thus the data for this study was collected after meeting 333 single women as against the target of 372. With increasing education and employment opportunities it became considerably more difficult to interview the required sample of non-working spinsters.

(iii) Sampling Procedure

The random sampling technique was used to draw the sample for the study using the random digit technique.

A thirty per cent sample of the establishments were taken to draw working respondents for interviews. For selecting the establishments for the study, a list of establishments first in both the public and private sectors employing more than 50 women was collected from the Directorate of Employment and Training, Bangalore. This was because the probability of finding single women in such organisations was higher. From this list a 30% representative sample of establishments, Central Government, State Government, Semi Government was identified. Of these 83 were classified as Government establishments and 56 were classified as private establishments. From these establishments working respondents were drawn using the random technique.

In case of non-working respondents, the absence of data base led the researcher to interview them on a purposive basis. Organisations having contact with single women were visited, such as social welfare organisations both government and private, matrimonial bureaux. Lawyers dealing with matrimonal cases were contacted and records of courts were looked into to get a list of unmarried and divorced women.

The state treasury was also visited in order to get a list of widows drawing a pension from the state government. Contact through friends and relatives also helped the researcher to meet many single non-working women.

To get an adequate representation of single women from the various socio-economic backgrounds the different zones in the city as classified by the Bangalore City Corporation were visited. This helped in getting a better perspective of the problems faced by the various groups of single women.

Visits to working women's hostels, state owned reception centres, homes run for destitute women, remand homes, and slums helped the researcher to draw a sample from the middle and lower economic strata of society.

The Questionnaire A structured questionnaire was developed and used as a tool for collecting information regarding the profile and problems of single women. The questionnaire has two parts. Part A deals with the demographic character and information on the family and the socio-economic background of the single women. Part B deals with causes for their remaining single, their problems and their status as perceived by them, their families and society. Questions pertaining to their attitude towards several institutions like remarriage, adoption, etc., were also included.

Pilot Study and Field Work. After preparing a very comprehensive questionnaire a pilot study on a representative sample of single women was made. Simultaneously copies of the questionnaire were sent to experts in the field of women's concerns for their comments and suggestions.

On the basis of the analysis of the pilot study and the suggestion made by the experts the questionnaire was modified and refined.

During the course of field work it was found that the interview method was most suitable as it provided scope to get in-depth insight into women's problems. However with respondents who were willing and educated, the questionnaire method was also adopted to elicit information.

Statistical Techniques used for the Analysis of Data. The present study was undertaken with the main purpose of studying in detail the problems of single women. With this purpose in view, it was not important to go into sophisticated statistical analysis, as such. Simple percentages were used to draw inferences. The descriptive method of analysis was found to be most appropriate.

(iv) Limitations of the Study

In this connection it would not be digressing to enumerate the difficulties faced by the researcher while interviewing the respondents.

At the outset many establishments could not be located and a few had been closed. A majority of both Government and private establishments showed a definite reluctance to furnish the list of single women or to accord permission to interview them. The authorities felt that such information was highly sensitive and would encroach upon the personal and private life of their employees.

After a lot of persuasion and clarifying on the need for such data in bringing about socio-economic legislative measures to alleviate the suffering/exploitations of single women and to create a public opinion against such suffering the researcher was allowed to interview them.

At the respondents' level again they were assured that the information collected from them would be treated as strictly confidential and used only for the purpose of research.

It should be placed on record that some establishments were

very co-operative and evinced keen interest in persuading some of their reluctant single women employees to give information.

Respondents were interviewed both at the place of work and their residence. It was observed that those interviewed at the place of work gave relatively more reliable information, than those at their homes. The home environment seemed to have a confining effect on the respondents. Many respondents evaded interviews and some who gave appointments for interviews later gave excuses for cancelling them. Greater difficulty was experienced inducing the educated working women to cooperate than in inducing the non-working. Being a delicate subject, the time for interview ranged between 45 minutes and an hour. In certain cases several visits of this duration were necessary to induce respondents to give information. This necessitated the researcher building a good rapport so as to draw the respondents into a mood to talk freely and truthfully. Several respondents found this an opportunity to reduce their own tensions by talking to the researcher. They took more time and discussed a lot of other issues which were not directly related to the study. This required a lot of insight to listen and cull out such information as was pertinent to the study.

Widows belonging to the lower strata of society expected financial assistance while spinsters wanted to know whether the researcher would open a matrimonial bureau to find a match for them. The most indifferent of the lot were divorced or separated women who often put up a wry face and showed open resentment.

Sympathetic treatment and a human approach towards understanding their problems invariably helped the researcher to establish a favourable rapport and thus interview them. Many women broke down and wept uncontrollably while some cursed the researcher for having opened up closed memories regarding their sufferings.

In summary it can be said that data collection for this study was indeed a very difficult task. The points highlighted above explain the problems faced by the researcher, and the inability to follow a strict sampling procedure. Under such circumstances the limitations of the study are obvious.

3

Profile of Working and Non-Working Spinsters

(i) Demographic Details

In this chapter, an outline of the profile and attitudes of working and non-working spinsters is drawn. It includes an examination of their demographic back-ground, religion, caste, marital and occupational status. The family back-ground and the educational index of the members of the parents' family, and that of their current families is also outlined. The economic status of their parents, their attitude towards the other spinster members of their families, and the reaction of spinsters to such attitudes are discussed. The problems faced by them at work, at home, and in society, their reactions to such problems, and methods adopted to overcome them are also discussed.

A majority of the working spinsters (66%) are aged between 35 to 40 years. While 19% of them are in the age group of 41 to 45 years, only 15% are above 46 years.

Even among non-working spinsters a majority come in the age group of 35 to 40 years (61%), 31% of the respondents are between 41 to 45 years only 8% of them are above 46 years of age.

It is seen that the majority of the respondents from both the categories are below 40 years and hence may be considered relatively young.

Place of Birth and Migration. Among the working spinsters though 82% were born in urban areas it is significant to note that 98% of them have lived for the most part of their lives in urban areas and hence have had urban upbringing. Table S.I.

As regards the place of birth it is seen that the majority of the respondents are from Karnataka (81%). 12% of the respondents are from the neighbouring states of Kerala, Tamilnadu and Andhra Pradesh, and the remaining 7% have migrated from countries like Burma, West Pakistan, etc.

Of the 81% who were born in Karnataka, the intra-state migration rate reveals that 64% of the respondents were born in Bangalore city alone and only 36% have migrated from within the state. While migration from within the state has mainly been of the rural-urban nature that from outside the state/country has been urban-urban migration.

Migration might have been due to the apparent availability of education and employment opportunities in Bangalore city.

As regards the non-working spinsters, it is seen that 92% of them were born in urban areas while 96% have spent most of their lives in urban areas. Table S.1.

Data regarding the place of birth of the respondents indicates that 96% are from Karnataka state, and of them 87% are from Bangalore city alone. Only 13% have migrated from different parts of the state both rural and urban.

Inter-state migration is only 4%, i.e., from Uttar Pradesh.

Thus it is seen that the majority of both the working and non-working spinsters have had an urban background coupled with an urban upbringing.

Religion and Caste (Working and non-working). A religion-wise analysis of working and non-working spinsters indicates that Hindus form the largest group 86% and 91% respectively followed by Christians, 11% and 9% and Muslims 3% and nil. Among the Hindus in the working group Brahmins form the predominent caste (52%) followed by scheduled caste with a proportion of 11%; Vokkaliga, Naidu, Reddy and Mudaliar form 11%. Of the remaining 9%, 3% belong to Vysha community and 2% each to Kstriya, Kankari, Pillai etc (6%). 3% of the respondents are not willing to disclose their caste/community. Among the non-working, Brahmins again form the predominent group

TABLE S.1

Distribution of the Working and Non-Working Spinsters by Place of Birth and Place Lived for Most Part

Sl. No.		Type of Spinster	Total	%	Total	%	Total	%
				Rural			Urban	
1.	Place of Birth	Working Spinster	11	18%	51	82%	62	100%
		Non-working Spinster	2	8	21	92	23	100
2.	Lived for the most part	Working Spinster	1	2	61	98	62	100
		Non-working Spinster	1	4	22	96	23	100

74% followed by Gowda 13% and other castes like Tiwari 4%, etc. Table S 2.

TABLE S.2

Castewise distribution of the working and non-working Spinsters

		Working Spinster		*Non-working Spinster*	
Sl. No.	*Caste*	*Total*	*%*	*Total*	*%*
1.	Brahmin	32	52	17	75
2.	Vokkaliga, Naidu, Reddy, Mudaliar	7	11	—	—
3.	Scheduled caste	7	11	—	—
4.	Gowda	—	—	3	13
5.	Catholic	4	7	1	4
6.	Protestant	3	5	1	4
7.	Sheik, Sunni Syeda	2	3		
8.	Not willing to disclose caste	2	3		
9.	Others	5	8	1	4
10.	TOTAL & %	62	100	23	100

W Spinster other :—	T	%
Kstriya	1	2%
Konkini	1	3%
Pillai	1	2%
Vysha	2	3%

NW Spinster Other :—	T	%
Tiwari	1	4%

Educational qualification of the respondents. An analysis of the educational qualification of the working respondents shows that the majority of them are highly educated, i.e., post graduates

TABLE S.3

Educational qualification of the working and non-working spinsters

Sl. No.	Educational qualification	Working spinster		Non-working spinster	
		Total	*%*	*Total*	*%*
1	Illiterate	—	—	—	—
2	Literate without formal education	—	—	1	4
3	Lower primary (1 to 4th) standard	1	2	1	4
4	Upper primary (5 to 7th) standard	1	2	2	9
5	High school education (8 to 10th) standard	17	27	9	39
6	Inter/P.U.C.	6	10	4	18
7	Graduate	15	24	5	22
8	Post-graduate	19	30	1	4
9	Technical/Professional	3	5	—	—
	TOTAL & %	62	100	23	100

30%, graduates 24% and 5% of the respondents have either technical or professional qualifications. 10% of the respondents are intermediates and 27% are matriculates, only 4% of the respondents have upper primary education. Table S.3.

Among the non-working spinsters the majority of them 36% are matriculates, 26% are either graduates or postgraduates, 18% are intermediates and 13% have either lower primary or upper primary education. 4% of the respondents did not receive any formal education.

Thus while 69% of the working respondents are intermediates and above, among non-working spinsters the proportion is only 44%.

It is surprising to note that there are spinsters who are educated and not working, either because they are unable to find suitable jobs or because of family restrictions. Table S.3.

Occupation, years of service and monthly income of the working spinsters. The majority of the working spinsters are employed as clerical staff in either the public or the private sector (37%), 21% are in the teaching profession, 10% in the nursing profession and 18% are production workers in factories or private firms. Only 14% of the respondents are working at the managerial or executive level.

It is significant to note that although quite a high proportion

TABLE S.4

Occupation of the Working Spinsters

Sl. No.	*Present Occupation*	*Total*	*%*
1.	Teacher	13	21
2.	Doctor/Engineer	—	—
3.	Nurse	6	10
4.	Salaried official	9	14
5.	Clerical staff	23	37
6.	Ayah/Peon/Attendant	—	—
7.	Pvt. firm/worker in a factory	11	18
8.	Bathi roller/Tailor	—	—
9.	Others	—	—
	TOTAL & %	62	100

of respondents hold post graduate degrees, they are not placed in correspondingly high jobs and are therefore under-utilized. Table S.4.

As regards the number of years of service it is seen that 32% of the respondents have been working between 11 to 15 years, 24% between 16 to 20 years, 16% between 21 to 26 years and about 28% for 10 years and less.

Thus while 60% of the respondents have less than 15 years of experience, 40% of them have put in more than 15 years of service. These figures are related to the age-profile, whereas 66% of the respondents are between 35 to 40 years.

Most of the spinsters (66%) earn an income of Rs 1001 to Rs 2501 and above per month. While 18% earn between Rs 501 and 1000 per month 16% of the respondents earn Rs 500 or below per month. Table S.5.

TABLE S.5

Monthly Income of Working Spinsters

Sl. No.	*Monthly income*	*Total*	%
1.	Retired	—	—
2.	Nil income	—	—
3.	Rs 1 to 300	9	14
4.	Rs 301 to 500	1	2
5.	Rs 501 to 1000	11	18
6.	Rs 1001 to 2000	28	45
7.	Rs 2001 to 2500	7	11
8.	Rs 2501 and above	6	10
	TOTAL	62	100

Working spinsters with post graduate qualifications who were employed as clerks or assistants in public sector undertakings like banks, or Life Insurance Company with considerable years of service earned between Rs 1000 to 2500 per month.

A large number of those in the teaching profession who were trained post graduates employed in the government schools with long years of experience were found to be earning less than those employed in either banks or the Life Insurance Company. However, those graduates or post graduates employed in private schools earned less than their counterparts in government schools inspite of their long years of experience. Those employed in the private sector were found to be earning less than Rs 800 per month.

Thus on an average, the majority of the working respondents have put in many years of service and are therefore earning a moderately high income.

Their economic independence and financial security may be one of the reasons for their decision to remain single.

Type of Family. A vast majority of working spinsters (71%) live in nuclear families while 24% live in joint families. Only 5% live independently in hostels.

Among the non-working spinsters 66% of them are from nuclear families. 17% from joint families and the rest, 17% are residing in state-owned reception centres, homes for destitute women or hostels. Thus it is observed that a relatively higher proportion of non-working spinsters are dependent on the joint family and centres for the protection of destitute women. Employed women on the other hand seem to be either living in nuclear families or independently.

Family Background. Education, occupation and monthly income of the parents have been taken into account for analysing the family background of the respondent.

An analysis of the family background of the working spinsters reveals that the majority of the respondents' fathers are matriculates, 42%. 21% have had either graduate or post graduate education, 11% professional or technical education and 8% have had intermediate education (P.U.C.) while 11% are educated up to the upper primary level, a negligible 2% are illiterates. 5% of the respondents did not disclose information regarding the education of their fathers.

The educational pattern of the non-working spinsters' fathers reveals that 39% of them are graduates, 4% have either professional or technical education, another 4% of the respondents' fathers have had upper primary and 9% high school education, while 13% are illiterates. Education of 31% of the cases is not available.

A comparison of the education of the fathers of the working and non-working spinsters reveals the following 3 points :

(i) A higher proportion of the fathers of non-working spinsters have a qualification of graduation and above (43%) than those of working spinsters (32%).

(ii) 50% of the working spinsters' fathers have Matriculation and Intermediate education as against only 9% of the non-working spinsters'.

(iii) While 13% of the fathers of the non-working spinsters are illiterates, the percentage is a negligible 2% for working spinsters.

From the above it is observed that in general the fathers of working spinsters have acquired more education than the fathers of non-working spinsters.

82% of working spinsters' fathers have high school and above as compared to only 52% among the non-working spinsters.

An occupation-wise analysis shows that 31% of the fathers of working spinsters have retired from service while 25% of them are employed as salaried offlcials, businessmen or professionals. 14% are employed as salaried non-officials and 17% are employed as unskilled labour. In 13% of the cases information is not available.

For non-working spinsters the data pertaining to occupation of the fathers is not available in 30% of the cases. 22% of them have retired from service and another 22% are employed as businessmen, professionals and salaried officials while 13% are non-officials and unskilled workers.

Of those who are employed and earning an income, in view of their moderate education, 30% of the fathers of working spinsters are in the income range of Rs. 501 to Rs. 1000 p.m.

24% earn below Rs. 500 p.m. and only 10% more than Rs. 1001 p.m. 22% are retired and information is not available in 14% cases.

The income of non-working spinsters' fathers shows that they fall mainly in the Rs. 501 to 750 range (26%), followed by those who earn below Rs. 500 p.m. (18%). Information for 30% of the cases is not available and 22% are retired. 4% earn above Rs. 1000 per month. As the majority 26% are employed in low income generating jobs, it is not surprising that they earn less.

Conclusion. Thus the proportion of fathers of working spinsters who have acquired education and are able to earn more is higher than that of the non-working spinsters' fathers.

Of the working respondents' mothers, 35% have had primary education. A significant number of them, 35%, are illiterates, 21% are educated up to the high school level and 7% are either graduates or post graduates. Education of the respondents' mothers is not known in 2% of the cases.

As regards the educational qualification of the mothers of non-working spinsters, it is seen that the majority of them 57% have had primary education, 17% are illiterates. None of them are matriculates. Only 4% are graduates. Information is not available in 22% of the households

Regarding the occupation of the mothers of both working and non-working spinsters almost all of them are housewives. As such they were non-earning members of the family.

In general the working spinsters' parents have acquired education to a greater extent than those of non-working spinsters. However, even the parents of the non-working spinsters have provided education to their children to a higher level than themselves. This indicates higher educational mobility among the respondents. This is further evinced from an examination of the family educational index that has been developed below.

For calculating the educational index of the family the following weightages were given to each level of education :

Level of education		*Weightages*
Less than 10th Standard	...	1
Matriculation	...	2
College Education (PUC)	...	3
Graduation	...	4
Post graduation	...	5
	Total	15

Based on the break-up of these weightages the households were categorised as less educated, moderately educated and highly educated households.

The first category consisted of households[1] whose total score ranged between 1 to 4. Such households are grouped as less educated households. In such households the majority of the members of the household have less than high school education. Secondly, households whose score ranged between 5 and 7 were grouped under moderately educated households. The majority of the members of such households are either matriculates or intermediates. Finally, households scoring a weightage of 8 and above were grouped as highly educated households. The majority of the members in these households have an education up to the graduation level and beyond. These households were grouped and percentages were calculated to derive the educational index of the family. This index has been used to find out the proportion of families (both parental and current) of the spinsters in each of the categories.

Educational index of the parental family. 89% of the households[1] of the parents' family of the working spinsters belong to the highly educated group and 11% to the moderately educated group. None of the households fell in the less educated

[1]'households' here means all the other members of the family, excluding the parents and the respondents. The parents' and respondents' education has already been dealt with.

group. This indicates that the majority of the members of the parents' families have a high level of education.

For the non-working spinster, 70% of the households of the parents' side belong to the highly educated group. Only 13% of the households belong to the less educated group and 13% to the moderately educated group. Information is not available for 4% of the households.

Thus it is observed that 100% of the members of the parental families of working spinsters are either highly or moderately educated as against 83% in non-working spinsters' households. Again, while there are no households among the working spinsters who fall in the less educated group, the percentage is 13 for the non-working spinsters' households.

Educational index of the family in which the respondent is currently residing. In the working spinsters' households the majority of the members seem to have a high level of education. It is seen that 64% of the households belong to the highly educated group of households. 23% of the households belong to the moderately educated group of households and only 13% of the households belong to the less educated group of households.

While among the non-working spinsters, 61% of the households belong to the highly educated group of households, 39% are from the less educated group of households and none is in the moderately educated group of households.

In conclusion a comparison of the educational index of the working and non-working spinsters reveals that the educational level of the working spinsters, their parents, families and their current families is much higher than that of non-working spinsters, their parents, families and their own.

Financial status of the parental families and families in which the respondents are currently residing. To analyse the financial status of the families the poverty line has been used as a norm. Information collected from the 7th Five Year Plan 1985-90 from the planning department Government of Karnataka fixes the poverty line by consumption pattern, for the year 1983 as Rs. 532 for urban industrial workers. This has been taken as the demarcating line to group the families by income and categorise them as those below the poverty line and above the poverty line. Since most of the respondents interviewed for the study are employed in the organised sectors of the economy where wages and conditions are regularised, not much variation was noticed between their wages and that of industrial workers. As such the per capita income per month for industrial workers (Rs. 532) has been taken into account for all the three groups. However, it is necessary to mention a very important limitation of the study. Information pertaining to workers from only organised sectors has been taken into account, omitting those workers in the unorganised sectors.

To calculate the per capita income of the family the total income and size of the family has been taken into account. Those households which cannot afford an average expenditure of Rs. 130 per month per member of the family are defined as "below the poverty line" (1983 prices).

Judged from the above standards it is seen that 52% of the respondents parents' families are above the poverty line, and 45% of the households are below the poverty line. Information is not available for 3% of the households. In the families where the respondent is living, the majority of the households (65%) are above the poverty line and 35% of them are below the poverty line.

It is seen that as regards the non-working spinsters, the majority of their parental families (48%) are below the poverty line and only 35% are above the poverty line. 17% of the respondents have not furnished this information.

In the households where the respondent is currently residing it is seen that 61% of the families are below the poverty line and 26% are above poverty line. Information is not available in 13% of the households.

The above data reveals that the per capita income of both parental and current families of working spinsters is higher than that of non-working spinsters. Again it is observed that there is an upward mobility, from below to above the poverty line in the parental to current families among working spinster households, while among the non-working spinsters' households there is downward mobility.

Per capita income is the function of the family size. Based on the total number of family members the households were categorised into 3 groups. A family comprising of 4 members was considered as a small size household, that of 5 to 8 members as the medium size, nine and above as large size families.

Based on this an analysis of the family of working spinsters from the parents' side indicates that 60% of the families belong to the medium size households and 19% each belong to small (1 to 4 members) and large size households, respectively.

In the families where the respondent is residing at present it is seen that an almost equal proportion of households 45% and 42% belong to small size and medium size households. Only 13% of them are from large size families. 43% of the parental households of non-working spinsters belong to small size households while 35% are from medium size households. 9% belong to large size households. Information is not available in 13% of the households. Even in the households where the respondent is residing at present it is seen that 48% of each of the households belong to either small or medium size households only 4% are from large size families.

A comparison of the parental and current family size of the spinsters reveals that while a higher proportion of households among those who are working belong to the medium and large family group those among the non-working group are from small size families.

However, there is a higher per capita income in working spinsters' households than non-working spinsters' households. This may be due to the following two reasons.

(i) The numbers working and the total family income inspite of the large family size, is high when compared to the non-working.

(ii) Inspite of the small sized families of the non-working spinsters the per capita income is low due to a fewer number of working members and due to their being employed in low paid jobs.

Assets. The financial status of the family can be further judged by the number and the value of assets that these families possess.

An index has been developed for estimating the worth of the assets and consequently the family's position. The weightages given to the assets that were considered are as follows :

House—9	TV—4
Land/site—8	Gas—3
Car—7	Fan—2
Fridge—6	Bicycle—1
Scooter—5	

The sum of all these weightages was taken as 45 and cut off points were arrived at to group households as low, medium and high asset group households.

Households having a value of 15 and below were grouped as the low asset group households, in other words, the assets owned by these families are relatively low.

Households scoring a value between 16 and 30 were grouped under medium asset group households. Such households owned modestly good assets.

Those households with a value of 31 and above were classed as the high asset group households that is these households have a sizeable number of assets to their credit.

And finally households not having any of these assets mentioned above were categorised as zero or nil asset group households. An important observation was made while analysing the data on assets. Information pertaining to assets are individually based and some people were not willing to disclose their assets and so there is some under or over estimates in the data.

An analysis of the assets of working spinsters' families shows that an equal proportion of the households from the parents' family (47%) and those where the respondent is residing at present (47%) fall under the medium asset group households. Only 13% of the households from the respondents' parents' family and 11% of the households in which the respondent is staying at present seem to own a large number of assets. A significant point to be noted is that 40% of the parental families and 42% where the respondent is residing at present belong to either low asset group households or those who possess no assets.

43% of the parents' families of non-working spinsters belong to either no or low asset group households and 39% belong to that of the medium asset group, only 18% belong to the high asset group.

Asset possession of the families reveals that among both groups while there is no difference in the percentages of medium and high asset holders there is an increase in the proportion of low asset households. This might probably be due to the reduction in the proportion of spinsters in the nil asset group.

Comparing the two groups a higher proportion of working spinsters belong to the medium and high asset group than non-working spinsters do. This indicates a slightly better financial position among working spinsters.

The financial status of the working respondents' families further shows that in view of their better financial status 76% of them have not taken any loan. Only 24% have taken the loan, the reasons being basically for productive purposes and long term investments like house construction, repairs, business, etc. A few have taken loans either for domestic expenditure or for the marriage of their sibblings. The amount of loan taken varies from less than Rs. 1000 to Rs. 30,000. The loans are generally taken from their place of work (73%) with a nominal rate of interest. In case of non-working spinsters most of them have not taken (96%) and only one respondents (4%) reported taking a loan of below Rs. 1000 for domestic expenditure.

Working spinsters because of their secure finances are able to save as it is seen that 84% of them have savings and only 16% do not have any savings. In the case of non-working spinsters they are not able to save much as is seen from the fact that 83% of them did not report any savings and only 17% reported savings.

Among working spinsters, of those who saved, when asked as to whom they propose to nominate as heir to their savings the majority said they have nominated their family members as their immediate heir (brothers, sisters, nephew, nieces) (61%). 15% planned to donate their savings to orphanages or towards charity and 6% to religious organisations. 2% who intended to get married considered their children as heir to their savings.

TABLE S.6

Proposal regarding nomination of heir among Non-working spinsters.

Sl. No.	Nominations	Total	%
1	Brother	2	9
2	Orphanages	1	4
3	Religious organisations	1	4
4	N.A./No savings	19	83
	Total	23	100

Proposal regarding nomination of heir among working spinsters.

Sl. No.	Nominations	Total	%
1	Family members	38	61
2	Orphanages	9	15
3	Religious organisations	4	6
4	To children when they get married	1	2
5	No savings	10	16
	Total	62	100

An enquiry about the heir to their savings among non-working spinsters reveals that the majority of them (9%) wanted to nominate their brothers and the remaining 8% wanted to donate their savings to either orphanages or religious organisations.

Since most of the respondents (44%) are at present staying with their brothers' family they obviously want to leave their savings to them. 17% of the respondents are staying with their parents, 13% with a single parent or sisters and another 13% are staying in state owned reception centres, or a home for destitute women or hostels. 9% of the respondents are staying independently and only one respondent 4% is residing in a hostel.

Thus the financial condition of the non-working spinsters' households is much lower when compared to that of working spinsters. Most of them are dependent on their families for their financial needs and as such very few respondents seem to be financially self-sufficient.

Expenditure Pattern of Working Spinsters. Though a large number of working spinsters (66%) earn an income of Rs. 1001 to Rs 2501 per month, yet the expenditure incurred on self reveals that the majority of them (77%) spend less than Rs 200 per month on themselves. Regarding expenditure towards maintenance of the family 50% of them spend Rs 201 to Rs 500 per month. 35% of them contribute more than Rs 500 per month. Most of them do not spend any amount on friends or relatives (85%) and a few spend between Rs 51 to Rs 100 per month.

The income that the working spinsters earn seems to be a major source of income to their families. They spend little or less on themselves than on relatives or friends. Table S.7. This may be because most of the spinsters are residing either with their parents (45%), or a single parent, relatives and other members of the family (36%) (brother or sister) only 19% of them are staying independently. This expenditure pattern is responsible for the vast majority of working spinsters' savings pattern (84%).

TABLE S.7

Expenditure Pattern of the Working Spinsters

Sl. No.	Amount in Rs.	Expenditure on Self		Contribution to the maintenance of family		Expenditure on Relatives		Expenditure on Friends	
		Total	*%*	*Total*	*%*	*Total*	*%*	*Total*	*%*
1	Less than Rs. 50	8	13	Nil	Nil	3	5	6	10
2	Rs. 51 to Rs. 100	12	19	6	10	3	5	21	34
3	Rs. 101 to Rs. 200	28	45	3	5	2	3	5	8
4	Rs. 201 to Rs. 500	14	23	31	50	1	2	—	
5	Rs. 501 to Rs. 1000			22	35	—	—	—	—
6	Total	62	100						
7	Nil Expenses	—	—			53	85%	30	48
						Total 62	100%	62	100

Marital status of family members in spinsters' households. The number of females above 35 years including the respondent and their marital status was collected to see how many other members in the family are single. An analysis of this data shows that in the households of working spinsters a significant number of females including the respondent (54%) are not married as against only 46% of the married females.

Though many of the females have received education and are employed and earning an income they are not married. Most of them seemed to have remained single out of choice. Perhaps they do not look at the institution of marriage as a necessity. This may be due to their exposure to certain unhappy social realities. Besides, their own psychological needs of recognition and social status might have been met, thus making them consider marriage as not an institution which provides these.

Analysis of the material status of the other members of the family including the respondent in the non-working group shows that 57% of the females above 35 years are unmarried as against 43% who are married. Family circumstances, financial constraints, and a combination of these factors seem to have influenced a large number of females to remain single. Very few respondents have remained single out of choice.

While there is no significant difference in the proportion of unmarried females in working spinsters' households there is a difference in the reasons for remaining single. A greater number of women in working spinsters' households are single out of choice than in non-working spinsters' households.

Reasons for remaining single. An analysis of the reasons for remaining single shows that among working spinsters family circumstances, personal choice and a combination of these factors have influenced the respondents' decision to remain single. 47% of the working spinsters have remained single out of choice. While 31% of them have cited family circumstances the remaining (22%) have given both the reasons of personal choice and family circumtances.

Family circumstances and financial constraints in the family have forced a high proportion of respondents to remain single. An indepth analysis of circumstances in the family which have come in the way of the respondents' marriage indi-

TABLE S.8

Reasons for remaining single among working and non-working spinsters

Sl. No.	*Reasons for remaining single*	*Working spinsters*		*Non-working spinsters*	
		Total	%	*Total*	%
1	Family circumstances	19	31	8	35
2	By choice	29	47	6	26
3	Or both the reasons	14	22	9	39
	Total	62	100	23	100

cates that the majority of them 38% have not married due to problems of dowry or because the groom desires a girl who is in a high salaried job (38%). The second major reason has been the lack of good parental background. Parents of respondents who have had intercaste marriages were unable to find a suitable groom within their respective castes as they were often not accepted (21%).

Having irresponsible fathers who either gambled or were addicted to drinking and/or brothers who did not take sufficient interest in finding a marriage partner has forced 16% of the respondents to remain single.

The early death of the parents and the need to educate younger sibblings have forced 10% of the respondents to remain single while another 10% have to look after children of their widowed sisters and have therefore not married.

The rest, 5%, are not married because their elder sisters are still unmarried.

Although the working spinsters are financially better placed than the non-working spinsters, it is surprising to note that the problem of dowry is one of the main problems for remaining unmarried

This is aptly described by Dr. Promilla Kapur in her article in *Femina* (June 23, July 7, 1985) where she cited that "when even an economically independent girl gets married in most cases a demand for dowry is expressed by the boy's parents. If these girls do not bring adequate dowry, dowry deaths are known to occur. Thus the impact of a girl's economic independence, has not removed the social evil of dowry from society."

Perhaps the recurring income from their employment is not considered as sufficient dowry by the bridegroom's family. Further she states, "In most cases a woman is allowed by her husband and even in-laws, to work. Research studies have strongly supported that 86% of the husbands wanted, or did not mind if their wives worked, and continued in their jobs or career after marriage. Even the older generation of the in-laws approved of their daughters-in-law working."

Under such circumstances it is no wonder there is a great demand for girls in good jobs with high salaries in the marriage market and consequently girls with low paid jobs are not given preference by most of the grooms.

Under such circumstances it is possible to conclude that perhaps the greed for dowry from the groom's family is so high that even people with high salaried income find it difficult to satisfy their initial and continuous demands.

Reasons for Remaining Single. The reasons for remaining single for non-working spinsters reveal a contrasting picture. The majority (39%) of the respondents have remained single due to both family circumstances and personal choice. 35% of the respondents have remained single out of family circumstances and 26% have done so out of choice.

The major circumstances in the family which have prevented the marriage of the respondents have been either the death of the parents, the irresponsibility of other members of the family (like widowed mother and brothers) in taking the initiative to find a partner or their inability to pay dowry (37.5%).

The next most important reason has been the failure to find a proper match within their caste (25%). The other reasons given are desertion by parents (12.5%) their shouldering the family responsibilities (12.5%) and their unemployed state (12.5%).

Of those who have remained single out of choice among working spinsters it is significant to note that 31% of them cited the problem of not being able to get a good match as the main reason. To quote Promilla Kapur, "Financially independent women find it troublesome to find a man better placed in the professional ruling than her, for women in senior positions the field is even more restricted." Another 31% prefer to be single and independent because they do not want any family responsibility. 10% of the respondents have remained single for, according to them, the problems of married women are more than those of unmarried. Ill health, lack of good looks, fear of consequent rejection or religious inclination or wanting to serve society are some of the other reasons for remaining single (20%). The rest, 8%, do not get married either because they want to look after their parents in their old age or their parents have objected to their undergoing inter-caste marriages.

Among non-working spinsters, of those who have remained

single out of choice the major reasons are the lack of interest in marriage and family life (33%), the fear of sex in marriage (17%), incurable disease (33%), and their inclination towards spiritual life (17%).

Both choice and family circumstances have played an equal part in influencing 22% of the respondents in remaining single, among working spinsters, and 39% among non-working spinsters.

Parents' death and the necess'ty of their supporting and maintaining the family both financially and morally has prevented 36% of the respondents from marrying.

29% of the respondents have remained single due to poverty coupled with their inability to raise dowry requirements. Though some of the respondents were interested in getting married they were forced to remain single because their families not only did not take sufficient interest in getting them married but also placed a taboo on their finding a groom for themselves.

Due to physical handicap or incurable diseases 14% of the respondents have not been able to find a marriage partner.

For 21% of the respondents various reasons operated. They either did not believe in arranged marriages or were spiritually inclined or being the only child were unable to find a groom willing to take care of them and their parents.

Thus working spinsters being highly educated and well employed have higher expectations from marriage. Perhaps they prefer to live alone than to have an unhappy married life with a wrong person. This might be reason enough for them to remain single by choice. This coupled with their economic independence might have given them the courage to take the decision of living alone.

Among non-working spinsters it is observed that circumstances like having irresponsible parents who neither looked for a groom nor allowed them to settle with a person of their choice prevented 34% of the respondents from getting married. 22% of the respondents explained that due to their dark complexion they were unable to get a suitable partner.

11% each of respondents remained single as they either could not meet the dowry requirements or had the responsibility of looking after younger brothers and sisters; they were spiritually inclined or because of the fear of opposition they might face by marrying a person of their choice belonging to a lower caste than their own.

In conclusion, while the reasons for remaining single are widely spread, it is observed that social conscience among the working spinsters is high. Thus though employed and earning an income, in principle most of them are against the system of dowry. Therefore, they prefer to remain single than to purchase a groom, as against non-working spinsters who remain single due to the forced circumstances of not being able to pay the dowry.

(ii) Attitudes

After having seen the reasons for remaining single among working and non-working spinsters it was felt necessary to investigate the attitude of these women towards the institution of marriage.

Attitude towards marriage. An analysis of the attitude of the respondents towards marriage reveals an interesting and contradictory picture. Although the majority of the working spinsters (47%) have remained unmarried out of personal choice, a higher proportion of them feel that marriage is absolutely essential for all women because of the companionship, security, status and position that it provides in society, leading to respectability and personal fulfilment of women. 42% of the respondents, however, view marriage as only a social obligation or a way of life. Some of them feel that marriage is an unnecessary obligation for economically independent women.

Among non-working spinsters the majority of them feel that marriage is a must for all women (78%) because of social security, moral protection and the respectability that women gain in society. Only 22% of the respondents feel that marriage is not a requirement for those who are economically independent. Many feel that marriage is a social bondage. The views and attitudes of working spinsters seem to have been largely influenced by their socio-economic background and the circumstances under which they live in society.

Further respondents were asked whether they were disappointed at not being married. Answers to this question revealed a mixed response. While 50% of the respondents were disappointed another 50% said that they were not disappointed at not being married. The disappointment at not being married is higher among non-working respondents (61%).

When asked to list down the circumstances under which the respondent felt disappointed the following reasons were listed :

(i) The marriage of friends of similar age group (42%);
(ii) The marriage of younger brothers and sisters in the family (23%);
(iii) The thought of a lonely old age without a companion (23%) ;
(iv) Social harassment and lack of companionship or respect and position in society (12%).

The circumstances for disappointment listed down by non-working spinsters are :

(i) Marriage among friends of her own age group (36%);
(ii) Marriage of sisters or brothers in the family (29%); or
(iii) the need for moral support when faced with various problems (21%) ;
(iv) Ill-treatment/desertion by family members (7%) ;
(v) or when lonely (7%).

The question as to whether there were advantages in remaining single roused a mixed response, while 38% of working spinsters answered in the affirmative the proportion is only 26% for non-working spinsters.

The advantages mentioned by the working respondents are independence and freedom from responsibility (80%) and freedom to pursue spiritual life (10%) ability to help family members (7%) and having no encumbrances after death (3%). Perhaps these 48% of the respondents are those that have remained single out of choice rather than family circumstances.

Freedom from responsibility (50%) freedom to pursue spiritual life (33%) and the ability to help family members (17%) are the advantages cited by non-working respondents.

Lack of financial security coupled with lack of social status in society perhaps makes them feel that a marriage is a must for all.

In general all the spinsters whether working or non-working agree on the point that the disadvantages of remaining unmarried over-ride the advantages, especially in a country like India. To quote Promilla Kapur, "Research on the changing attitudes of working women towards marriage indicates that with passage of time working women who previously objected to marriage now want to get married. They feel insecure and dissatisfied if they are unable to find ideal mates for themselves. In fact one of their ambitions is to have a husband, home and children."[1]

In conclusion it can be said that because of increasing education and economic independence more girls are asserting their freedom and the choice to choose a way of life. "Many years ago most Indian women got married without a single pre-marriage glance at their life partner. Educated women began to feel that they had to have a say in the choice of their matrimonial partner."[2] They also seem to expect a lot from marriage besides wanting intelligent, smart and well established husbands who can give them a certain amount of independence, to continue with their work so as not to impair their own identity. Perhaps the circumstances under which they work and their constant exposure to the outside world might have changed their attitudes. Besides, social conditions in society and the lack of status given to unmarried women makes them feel that a marriage is a must.

Working spinsters are more confident, pragmatic and realistic. They seem to have the courage to face and tackle the various problems in life alone.

Social Status in Caste/Community. In a traditional society like ours where women generally hold a low status irrespective of caste, creed and community, the position and status of single women is deplorable. However, evidence regarding the treatment meted out to them by their community people was col-

1. Promila Kapur, *Femina* June 23rd-July7, 1985.
2. Vimal Patil, *Femina* Nov. 23rd-Dec., 1985.

lected. A majority of the working spinsters (68%) agree that they have a low status in society. They feel that they are degraded and looked at with suspicion; often they are treated as social outcastes and viewed as promiscuous women. Therefore they are subjected to immense social harassment. Perhaps their failure to conform to the norms of society and their unconventional way of life and being single have led the society to harass them at every point. However 32% of the respondents feel that they are treated as equals with other married women.

A higher proportion of non-working spinsters (87%) feel that they have low status as compared to the working spinsters. Only 13% of them agree that they are treated equally with other married women. Respondents feel that they are commonly degraded as social outcastes to the point of suspicion and ill-treatment because of their single status.

It is interesting to note that a larger number of working spinsters talked of equal treatment in society than the non-working group. Perhaps economic independence and financial security gives working spinsters a better status in their families and the society unlike the non-working who are entirely dependent on others.

Social Interaction—Attendance and Participation in Social and Religious Functions. In view of the low status that spinsters have in society most of them do not have any social life. An analysis of their responses to the question as to whether they are invited to social and religious functions, the extent of their participation in such functions and the reasons for not attending such functions, reveals interesting results.

All the working spinsters interviewed reported being invited to both social and religious functions by relatives and friends. While 77% attend either social or religious functions or both, 23% do not attend either of the functions. Of those who attend, 75% attend both social and religious functions. While 19% attend only religious functions. About 6% only attend social functions.

As regards the attendance and participation of non-working spinsters in social or religious functions it is seen that 77% are invited to such functions 13% of respondents are those who stay in destitute homes and as such do not have a social life to which to be invited.

Of those who attend, it is observed that 75% attend only religious functions, 25% only social functions. None of the respondents attend both the functions.

It seems that a comparatively higher percentage of non-working respondents attend social functions than the working respondents. This might be due to their being economically inactive and therefore free to attend such functions as by attending such functions they hope to meet a life partner. Besides many of the spinsters belong to the older age group and perhaps do not mind attending such functions as they might be reconciled to their single status.

The participatory behaviour of the respondents in such functions reveals that it is more in the nature of attendance rather than participation. The reasons for not attending or participating in such functions reveals that their unmarried single status is the main contributory factor, followed by fear of social gossip, physical health and embarassment, in the said order.

Problems at home. As regards problems at home it is seen that many of the working respondents (43%) feel lonely, insecure, have the burden of financially maintaining the family and have to carry out household chores, apart from their work outside home and they feel lack of emotional companionship and consequent physical and mental agonies. 34% of the respondents complain of indifference, ill-treatment and conflicts with parents and others. The problem of temperamental adjustments and differential treatment because of their unmarried status leads to severe tensions at home resulting in a feeling of depression. They are treated as just income earning machines. Most of them inspite of their economic contribution feel that they are a burden to their parents. The expenditure pattern of this group also revealed that a higher proportion of income is contributed towards the maintenance of families, rather than themselves. 6% are burdened with the problem of education, marriage a d health of their younger sibblings. 2% of the respondents feel that they are obstacles to the marriage of younger sister and brother and in turn therefore a burden to their parents.

They also complain of being financially exploited by their family members and relatives 5%.

It is necessary to mention here observations of Promilla Kapur who says that "Among some lower middle class families instances of parents who do not want their working daughters to get married are known, merely because the money that she brings home would then stop coming in". She further states, Observations of scientific study indicate that some financially independent single women are exploited economically at home and sexually at their place of work. The data highlights that working spinsters are financially exploited by their families to a great extent, without socio-cultural and moral support.

About 10% of the respondents stated that they did not have any problems and were quite happy. Though the majority of the respondents remained single purely out of choice, it looks as though the parents of this group of respondents are not happy about the decision of their daughters. Perhaps this may be the reason for the frequent conflicts at home resulting in respondents feeling extremely lonely and insecure. This again proves that though women by choice prefer to remain single, family members in particular and society in general object to it. To quote Peta J. Stein, "The possibility that some people might actually choose to be single because they feel it would contribute to their growth and well-being to remain so is simply not believed possible."

Non-working spinsters on the other hand seem to face more problems than working spinsters because of two reasons. Firstly they are economically inactive, they spend more time at home and secondly because of their financial dependence. The majority of them complain of insecurity, financial dependency, uncertainty about their future and lack of moral support. About 35% complain of various problems like loneliness, frustration, dejection and financial dependency coupled with the problem of adjustment with other family members, etc. 8% complain of indifference and ill-treatment by family members. Perhaps the feelings of incompleteness and lack of security and physical satisfaction make them feel tense and irritable resulting in frequent quarrels in the family. The other members of the family make them feel that they are an economic burden on the family. In general they suffer from psycho-emotional problems and financial insecurity. While working spinsters are subjected to psychological problems the non-working spinsters have in addition economic paoblems.

Problems at Work. Though working spinsters display greater confidence and enjoy a better status because of their economic independence, yet they are subjected to harassment and victimisation at the place of work. Most of them feel that they are a subject of gossip usually directed and intended to hurt. 35% men colleagues often make passes at them and make advances with a sexual motive (16%). There is the tendency among colleagues to make inquisitive enquiries as to the reasons for their not being married. As already mentioned scientific studies indicate that financially independent women are exploited sexually at their place of work.

Married women at the work place form their own cliques and treat single women with an air of superiority (10%). This feeling of rejection by women colleagues gives rise to various psychological problems. The attitudes of male colleagues and married female colleagues deeply hurt single women who are highly sensitive. Most of them are indignant and feel that society has no right to interfere in their personal life because of their choice to remain single. Some respondents even complain of differences of opinion with superiors in their offices because of their own independent nature and consequent ill-treatment. They also complain that financially they are exploited at the workplace (5%). 2% of the respondents complained of physical inability, dependence on others and consequent feeling of neglect. However 32% of the respondents report that they did not face any problems at the place of work and that they are quite happy. All these women are found to be employed in organisations meant for women only.

Psychological Problems. The social condition and status of spinsters not being very high they seem to be harassed both by society as well as their family members. Under such circumstances it is natural that they suffer from numerous psychological problems. Almost all working respondents 90% complain of loneliness, insecurity, dejection and frustration in various combinations. Only 10% of the spinsters are happy and do not suffer from any psychological problem.

A majority of the respondents among the non-working spinsters complain of loneliness, mental insecurity, dejection and frustration 83%, while 13% of them are lonely. A negligible 4% of the respondents do not have any problems.

Non-working spinsters seem to be suffering psychologically to a greater extent than working spinsters because of their financial dependence and lack of career to keep themselves occupied.

In conclusion it can be said that although quite a high proportion of working spinsters have remained single by choice they seem to be suffering from a sense of loneliness and insecurity. Perhaps the difference of time in their decision and experience of remaining single is reflected in their present thinking.

As an exercise of looking back at their decision perhaps they feel that marriage is after all a necessity for every women in society, not only because of the inherent desire of every human being for companionship but also for emotional and social security. The deliberate efforts made by these spinsters and their anxiety to get their younger sisters married again reflects their retrospective thinking in terms of their own single status and therefore the importance of marriage.

Decision making in the family. Respondents were asked as to whom they consulted regarding their career or matters relating to the family, their personal life, buying or selling of goods in the family. Working spinsters seem to contribute a lot to the decision making in the family.

39% of the respondents consulted their parents when taking decisions regarding their career. 27% decided on their own. 21% consulted their brothers or sisters. A few consulted their friends (13%). Regarding family affairs 41% of the respondents decide in consultation with parents. 27% of them take decisions on their own, followed by their sibblings 19% and friends 13%. So also in matters relating to their personal life, it is seen that the majority of the respondents (39%) consulted their parents and 29% of them decide on their own and the rest either consult their brothers or sisters (19%) or friends (13%). Buying or selling important goods in the household is mainly done either in consultation with parents (39%) or themselves (29%) followed by kith and kin (19%) friends (13%).

The earning spinsters do involve their parents in deci ion making, but it is observed that a significant proportion take decisions on their own, especially where buying and selling is concerned or in matters involving themselves. This may be because of their economic status in the family and their financial situation.

Promilla Kapur rightly says that "A working women is well cared for and respected at home and usually consulted in all matters" (*Femina* June 23rd July 7th 1985).

As regards non-working spinsters, it is seen that their status in their families is not so higher. They do not have any decision making power either in matters relating to the family or their personal lives. Decisions are mainly taken in consultation with sibblings (39%), parents (26%), and jointly with parents and brothers (17%). While 9% of the respondents consult their friends another 9% decide for themselves. The same is also true in matters relating to their personal life or issues relating to buying or selling in the family. Financial dependence and their inability to contribute economically to the family income may perhaps be responsible for their low status.

Outings. As mentioned earlier, the majority of the spinsters attend both religious and social functions. But most of them prefer to attend religious functions rather than social functions. Of those who attend social functions like a marriage, it is seen that most of the spinsters go either with their sisters or brothers (42%) or friends (33%). About 10% are accompanied by their parents and 15% attend on their own. Even with regards to attending religious functions or visiting temples, it is seen that the majority of them depend on their sisters or brothers (39%) followed by friends (28%) and parents (11%)

in the said order. More attend religious functions on their own than social functions 22%. With respect to casual outings or shopping the majority of them seek the company of their friends followed by sibblings, parents and relatives in the said order. Quite a few respondents go on their own (15%, 16%).

Among non-working respondents as mentioned earlier 13% of them do not attend either social or religious functions because they are staying in homes for the destitute. Of those who attend functions the majority of them attend either with their sisters or brothers (46%). Here again during the course of the inter view it was revealed that accompaniment of sisters seems to be more than brothers followed by friends 31% and parents 8%. 15% of the respondents attend on their own.

Comparatively more non-working spinsters attend religious functions on their own (34%). With regard to shopping or casual outings most of them are accompanied by their sisters or brothers (44%). Quite a few respondents go on their own (35%) and the rest (21%) are accompanied either by their friends or parents.

In general it is seen that while most of the non-working respondents depend on some members of their family, working respondents seem to be more dependent on friends to accompany them.

One significant point to be noted is that a higher percentage of non-working spinsters shop alone (35%) when compared to working spinsters (15%). Those women remaining at home are used by their families to do shopping, mainly for daily marketing.

Leisu·e time activities. An analysis of the leisure time activities of the working spinsters reveals that 67% of them have reading as the main leisure time activity, the remaining 33% being engaged in other activities like stitching, knitting, handicrafts, sports, gardening, listening or learning music, indoor games, seeing movies or attending religious discourses, or visiting relatives, friends, etc.

As regards the non-working spinsters it is seen that while a majority of them indulge in stitching, knitting, embroidery or handicrafts (35%), 30% spend their time in listening to or teaching music, conducting yoga classes, tuition classes or attending religious discourses, 22% of the respondents spend their time in reading. 13% who are inmates in the destitute homes are engaged in its various activities.

While the major leisure time activity of non-working spinsters is handicrafts that of working spinsters is reading. Since the non-working spinsters are economically inactive they may find it personally satisfying to engage themselves in handicrafts or socially useful activities.

Future Plans. 56% of the working respondents do not intend to get married as against 52% non-working respondents. Corollary among working spinsters 44% have plans of getting married as against 48% of non-working respondents. A slightly higher number of non-working spinsters have plans of getting married than the working spinsters. The non-working spinsters not being economically active, may look at the institution of marriage as a source of economic security and social status and the working spinsters in view of the agonies experienced by them in society because of their single status look towards marriage for social security and status.

Women who do not have intentions of marrying are either those who belong to the older age groups or those who have remained single by choice rather than under family circumstances.

It is seen that among the working spinsters having no marriage intentions 52% have no particular plans for the future, except that of continuing in their current jobs. The remaining 28% either want to go abroad, have a change of job in order to brighten their prospects, become a social worker, a member of a religious organisation or render help to younger members in the family or to construct a house. Surprisingly 20% of the respondents have absolutely no plans for the future.

As regards non-working spinsters it is seen that 34% want to take up a job. 16% either want to start a music institute or become a member of a religious organisation. Without a career coupled with their economic dependence and emotional insecurity it is understandable that as high as 50% of them have not even visualised plans for their future.

TABLE S.9

Leisure Time Activities of Working and Non-Working Spinsters

Sl. No.	Leisure activities	Working spinsters		Non-working spinsters	
		Total	*%*	*Total*	*%*
1.	Reading	42	67	5	22
2.	Stitching, knitting, embroidery, handicrafts	5	8	8	35
3.	Attending religious discourses	2	3	3	13
4.	Sports	1	2	—	—
5.	Gardening	2	3	—	—
6.	Learning or teaching music/Yoga/Tuition	2	3	4	17
7.	Listening to music	2	3	—	—
8.	Indoor games	1	2	—	—
9.	Visiting relatives & friends	1	2	—	—
10.	Movies	3	5	—	—
11.	Attending literary functions	1	2	—	—
12.	Attending to Ashram or R.C. work	—	—	3	13
	Total	62	100	23	100

Adoption. Since loneliness in the major psychological problem that single women face, spinsters were asked whether they would like to adopt a child to overcome their feeling of loneliness or as a support for their old age. 95% of the working and 100% of the non-working spinsters were against adoption against only 5% working spinsters who approved of it. The reasons for their disapproval indicate that 49% did not wish to entangle themselves in a legal, social and morally binding additional responsibility. About 32% of them were just not interested in the idea of adoption itself, while 14% feel that it would be an additional financial burden. 5% feel that adoption would involve unnecessary emotional attachment which would be ultimately rejected by the child once it comes to know about its adoption. 2% of the respondents who have adopted children have done so either for support during their old age or to get over their feeling of loneliness. The opposition in these few cases has been either only initially or nil.

None of the non-working spinsters were interested in adopting a child. The major reason for this being their own financial dependency, and a few fearing rejection after the child is aware of its parentage.

Thus while working spinsters disapproved of adoption on the grounds of additional responsibility and the lengthy legal proceedings, the non-working spinsters did so due to their own financial insecurity.

Measures suggested for the protection of spinsters. In view of the low status meted out to spinsters and the problem they face in their homes, work place and society, the respondents were asked to suggest measures on the basis of their own experiences for the protection of single women in contemporary society.

The majority of the working spinsters have suggested the opening of homes for single women by the government on the lines of the old age homes (43%). 21% are apathetic about the government doing anything. As such, they feel that only their kith and kin should look after them. 18% of the spinsters feel that voluntary organisations can help the single women by opening hostels and thereby give protection to them. About 3% opine that government should provide financial help and

TABLE S.10

Measures suggested by the working spinsters to be adopted for the protection of single women

Sl. No.	*Measures*	*Total*	*%*
1.	Opening of single homes by the government on the lines of old age homes	27	43
2.	Government can't do anything, kith & kin should look after them	13	21
3.	Financial protection & help by the government	2	3
4.	Voluntary organisations can help single women by opening hostels	11	18
5.	Voluntary organisations can start a small scale industry & help them to earn	1	2
6.	Don't know/cannot answer	8	13
	Total	62	100

Measures suggested by the non-working spinsters to be adopted for the protection of single women

Sl. No.	*Measures*	*Total*	*%*
1.	Financial protection and help by government	7	30
2.	Government cannot do anything, kith and kin should look after them properly	2	9
3.	Single women who are jobless can be provided with jobs, suitable to their skills	3	13
4.	Voluntary organisations with the help of the government can help the single women by opening hostels	5	22
5.	Opening of single homes by government, on the lines of old age homes	4	18
6.	Old age pension by government	1	4
7.	Don't know/cannot answer	1	4
	Total	23	100

another 2% felt voluntary organisations should open small-scale industries to provide non-working single women avenues to make a living. Another 13% of the respondents were indifferent and made no suggestions.

The majority of the non-working spinsters have suggested the need for financial protection and help from the government (30%), 22% have suggested that voluntary organisations, with the government, should help single women by opening hostels and thereby provide protection to them. 18% have suggested the opening of homes while 13% have said that single women who are jobless should be provided with jobs suitable to their skills. 9% are apathetic about government doing anything in this regard. About 4% feel that government should give them an old age pension and the remaining 4% did not make any suggestion.

Conclusion. The overall conclusion that can be drawn from this is that both working and non-working spinsters agree that they are given a low status in society. Working spinsters because of their higher education, economic independence and financial security are better placed than non-working spinsters who are financially dependent on others for even their meagre needs.

Working spinsters are exploited at the place of work though they enjoy financial freedom and status at home. Non-working spinsters on the other hand are doubly exploited by both family members and society as a whole.

On the whole all spinsters agree about the essentiality of marriage in the socio-cultural context of Indian society.

Though education, and subsequent employment, and financial independence can provide a possible substitute to marriage, yet under certain circumstances the unmarried women has to face a lot of problems.

To quote, "Women cannot be happy without marriage mainly because of three types of reasons: they are those related to the problem of protection and living arrangements, biological and companionship needs and social pressures and criticisms.

While it appears that social pressures on the unmarried women are lessening, traditional living arrangements and needs for protection and companionship still present practical difficulties."[1]

(iii) Case Histories of Working and Non-working Spinsters

Introduction. The observations of the study could be best highlighted by juxtaposing the conditions and status of a few single women by making a case study of women who are representative of the whole class. The feeling of rejection, humiliation, depression and the ill-treatment meted out to single women can best be illustrated by an in-depth analysis of a few women. A few case studies are outlined below from both working and non-working groups with varying backgrounds to highlight the peculiar problems faced by them in particular and spinsters in general.

Working Spinsters—Case Study No. 1

46 year old Madumati is a tall, slim woman possessing ordinary features, employed as a high school teacher for the past 20 years She is a post-graduate degree holder and at the time of the interview she was drawing a salary of Rs. 2000 per month.

She belongs to a middle-class Hindu family of whom only the eldest is married. At present she is residing with her unmarried younger sister and mother. Her late father was also a post-graduate and worked as a teacher. Though he encouraged his children to acquire education in several aspects he was a very 'conservative' man. According to the interview he was highly irresponsible and never made efforts to select marriage partners for his daughters. Madumati feels that it was her elder sister's good fortune to have married, failing which she too would have been unmarried like all the younger sisters.

Asked about the reasons for remaining single, she said that the interplay of circumstances and her own attitude towards

1. Blumberg, Lois Rhoda and Dwarki, Leela—*India's educated women, options and constraints.* Hindustan Publication Corporation, India, Delhi 1980.

men were responsible for her being unmarried. Her family was large. Apart from her father being irresponsible he imposed restrictions on his daughters finding marriage partners for themselves. But on her part she never liked male chauvanism and therefore could not think of subordinating herself to any man. But she was skeptical about finding such a person who would be her equal and respect her feelings.

Thus family circumstances and choice seem to have played an important role in influencing the respondent to remain single. Asked about her views on marriage Madumati feels that marriage in a society like ours is a must for all women, not only because of the companionship it provides but also because of social security. She feels every woman should experience motherhood. Questioned as to whether there was any advantages in being single Madumati answered in the negative. She feels that there are more disadvantages than advantages in being single.

Regarding the problems she has to face as a spinster, Madumati says that at home she is financially exploited not only by her family members who earn more than her but also by her relatives who expect her to help them financially.

She feels it a great burden to do the household chores and manage the work outside. Psychologically she is lonely and miserable and longs for a companion (husband) who could give her moral, emotional and intellectual companionship.

As an employed women all her energies were centralised on work. However, even then she confessed to depression as often her married colleagues discuss their families in reference to husband and children.

The social status of unmarried women in their caste reveals that single women definitely have a low status. Though economic independence gives her some status in her family, outside she is not accorded a respectable position.

Being economically independent Madumati takes all decisions in the family herself. She maintains regular contact with a few of her close friends and is accompanied by them on outings.

Writing poems, reading literature, attending music, dance festivals or travelling are her major leisure time activities.

Regarding plans for the future Madumati has no plans in particular except to continue in her current job. She may, however, consider marriage for companionship if she meets the right person.

The case of Madumati is representative of spinsters who inspite of high education and economic independence feel distressed for having not married. This is mainly due to the social and parental pressures in society and family. It is rightly said by Peter J. Stain, "In our society adulthood and emotional maturity are held to be synonymous with marriage and parenthood. A good life is defined as the married life. Any choice of life style that leads a marriageable person away from the social obligation to settle down is considered wrong. The person who chooses singlehood is seen as immature at best or even self-destructive. The attitude prevails that those who remain single are deviant or in some way inadequate for an adult role."

With the existence of such an attitude very few alternatives are available for women outside marriage.

Working Spinsters—Case Study No. 2

Meena, a 38 year old spinster, is employed as a clerk in a government office. She comes from a large middle class Hindu family of 4 sisters and 3 brothers. She lost her father at an early age and as the eldest and only earning member in the family she considers it her moral duty to support her sisters and brothers.

Further, Meena could not get married because of the problem of dowry in their community. She says, "The demand made on the bride's parents in her community is very large". The bride is expected to bring a huge amount of cash besides gold ornaments and diamond earrings and silver articles. Under such circumstances it was impossible for her to think of marriage. To quote, "A few women inflict self sacrifice on themselves and refuse to be bound to wedlock because they find their parents cannot find a dowry for them or if they can it will land them in economic hardship for the rest of a life time."

As the sole earning member of the family without other avenues of income she finds it extremely difficult to make both ends meet. Besides, the responsibility of the education of her younger sisters and brothers was entirely hers. It was fortunate that she could perform the marriage of her younger sister with her relative who did not make any dowry demands.

To lead a respectable life in society, Meena considers marriage for women essential. As a single woman she has been exposed to several problems both at home and in the office. The dual burden of running the household and earning an income has affected her physical and mental health. She longs for a person who could share her responsibilities, support and guide her family.

At work she is often ridiculed by colleagues and constantly made to feel that being unmarried is a sin. Emotionally she feels a vacuum in her life and longs for companionship.

She confesses to dejection as generally she is treated as the "Man of the family" not a person. Insp.te of it she is morally bound to her family. Basically introvert by nature, Meena finds satisfaction in sacrificing all her time and energy working for the welfare of the other members of her family. Having no friends she rarely goes out. In her leisure time she reads or visits the temple. Her main aim in life is to see her sister and brothers well settled in life, unlike herself.

Working Spinsters – Case Study No. 3

Latha, a 41 year old spinster, is a confident, smart and intelligent woman. She holds a post graduate degree and has been employed as a manager in a nationalised bank for the last 7 years. She earns a salary of Rs 3000 per month. Born and brought up in Bangalore, Latha belongs to a highly educated and cultured family of two sisters and one brother of whom she stands third chronologically.

Extremely brilliant from childhood, Latha was throughout a rank holder in both school and college, besides being a good sports women. Her father is a retired government servant and is at present living with her brother who is a doctor by profession.

Latha's younger sister is also unmarried, largely because of Latha. She is working as a lecturer in a local college in Bangalore. Latha and this sister are extremely close to each other.

Asked about the reasons for being unmarried Latha reacted indignantly and in turn questioned me as to what was wrong in being unmarried? She says that she has remained single mainly by choice and has never felt economically and emotionally insufficient without marriage. According to her, "These days marrying a man is more of liability than an asset". Career conscious women who want to excel professionally should never marry as family life would be a hindrance in their achievement.

Once married Latha feels that women lose all their freedom, physical and economic and become slaves. Marriage restricts their mental growth and stunts their personality development. Marriage is a definite threat to one's career and leads to stagnation. She for one enjoys her work and derives immense satisfaction from work.

Besides, Latha strongly feels that happiness and marriage do not necessarily go together. Marriage does not ensure complete happiness in life. The problems of adjustments with in-laws often make life hell for married women.

Asked as to how she overcame parental pressures regarding marriage, Lata says that her father being an extremely liberal person never imposed his views on his children. Though he is disappointed at their choice to remain unmarried he is proud of their achievements.

As her parents are economically self-sufficient they do not expect any financial help from her. Further, as she and her sister live together they rarely feel lonely. They share the household chores and therefore do not face problems in combining household duties with work outside.

At the work place she has heard her colleagaes discuss her status but none dare to question her directly about this because of the responsible position that she occupies in her office. However, she gets highly offended when they remark on her moral character. Hurt at such remarks Lata stated, "It is impossible to lead my life to suit other people's needs in society".

Holding a top managerial position and commanding a certain respect and position in society, Latha is extremely independent by nature. She takes her own decisions though yet at times she does so in consultation with her sister.

Being an extrovert she has a large circle of friends who accompany her on outings, shopping and seeing movies, etc. She spends her leisure in reading, listening to music, movies or visiting friends.

Her further plans rule out the possibility of marriage. She intends to go abroad and settle down there.

Latha is one of those few single women who manage to defy the conventions and lead a life of their choice. Though such women are rare to find it is interesting to note there are women who no longer view marriage and family life as pre requisite to a happy existence. High education, sound economic position and, to a certain extent, her family background has been responsible for the confidence she has in leading the life of a single women.

Non-Working Spinsters—Case Study No. 1

Sujata is a 45 year old spinster who is educated up to the matriculation level. She belongs to a small middle class family of two brothers and an elder sister who are all married and settled abroad. Sujatha lost her mother when she was very young and till recently she was staying with her old father. At present she is residing with one of her sisters-in-law who could not accompany her husband abroad, due to her children's education.

Not being interested in education Sujatha spent most of her time in household chores and with her level of education it was not possible to get a decent job with a decent income. Further, her father's objection also prevented her from seeking employment. At present she regrets both. She says that being employed would have not only made her financially self sufficient but also kept her busy.

The reasons for remaining single reveal that initially she rejected several proposals for various reasons and later with advancing age it was difficult to get the right match. Though she holds herself largely responsible for her present status, yet in moments of distress she holds it against fate.

Sujatha does not seem to be happy. She had some freedom when her father lived. But at present she is totally dependent on her relatives.

She confessed that, "It is better to have married a wretched fellow than to lead a life of dependence." According to her, every girl dreams of a happy home, husband and children and that she is no exception. She feels extremely isolated and at times in a state of confusion and is utterly frightened of the thought of a lonely old age.

At home she is treated indifferently by her relatives who constantly make her feel unwanted. Being financially dependent on them for her needs she is subjected to much exploitation. She is forced to do all the household work and is rarely given credit for it. When she finds a little time she engages herself in knitting and handwork.

In view of the oppressive and unpleasant experience undergone, Sujatha feels that marriage is an absolute necessity for all.

Ill-treated by her family and deprived of status in society, she feels that it is a double curse to be single and economically dependent.

Asked about her future plans Sujatha includes the possibility of marriage if and when she meets the right person.

Non-Working Spinsters—Case Study No. 2

50 year old Nagamani is the only daughter of her parents. She has a younger brother who has voluntarily retired from the defence services and is settled in Bangalore. Nagamani lost her mother at an early age. The responsibility of looking after her younger brother and sick father fell on her shoulders. She even discontinued her education for a few years to nurse her father back to health and help her brother to study. She later completed her graduation but was prevented by her father from seeking employment as he did not feel the need for her to work. He also wanted his daughter to get married.

Without a mother, the pressures of looking after her father and the needs of a younger brother fell on her. Nagamani at 22 years itself was spiritually inclined. She did not want to be married nor have marriage and family. She was adamant about her decision though it distressed her father.

Her father's constant worry about her decision to remain single worsened his health condition. Before his death he made his brother her guardian. Having lost her father and immensely grieved, her spiritual inclination increased. She became a member of the Ramakrishna Ashram. She was greatly attracted by the teaching of the Great Master and found a lot of solace in it.

Her brother who had joined the defence services left her. Nagamani stayed in the house left by her father, pursuing a spiritual life. A part of the house was given on a rent of Rs 300. With this she managed to maintain herself.

She got her brother married to her close friend. But soon there was a change. When they returned to Bangalore to stay at home, her sister-in-law, who was once her friend, started ill-treating her and made her do all the household work. She was not given enough food. Being mild by nature, Nagamani tolerated all this. Now her brother and his wife not wanting to give her a share in the property constantly batter her with the hope that she will leave the house.

Nagamani's estimation of the value of the house is Rs 2 lakhs. Her brother and sister-in-law refer to her as a 'chronic spinster', having no moral support. Doing all the household work without any help or assistance has affected her health to the extent that once on her way to the Ashram she collapsed. She got well with the help of friends. It is on their advice she is now staying in a hostel to relieve herself from the cruel clutches of her sister-in-law and brother.

Today she is dependent on her friends. Asked about her future plans she says, "Though my father left me financially sound at present I am left at the mercy of a few well wishers". She has no regrets for being unmarried but she considers it a matter of right to get a share of the property to maintain herself.

Conclusion. The above case histories of both working and non-working spinsters with different backgrounds reveal that various pressures are responsible for the respondents' decision to remain single. While single women in general are burdened with many problems, the condition of non-working single women is totally depressing.

Henry Wordsworth Longfellow poetically describes the feelings and conditions of a single person in the following lines.

> "As unto the bow the chord is
> So unto man is woman
> Useless each without the other."

4

Profile of Working and Non-Working Widows

(i) Demographic Details

Introduction. The present chapter deals with the problems of widows. Unlike spinsters who never had an opportunity to enjoy the protection and security of living with a man, widows suffer agonies that are indeed pathetic. Having had a sheltered life with their husbands, the grief and personal tragedy and the social stigma that they suffer as a consequence of widowhood is enormous.

Apart from the social ostracism that is imposed on them the emotional and economic crisis that they undergo in reorganising their lives to change in the family and social relationships affects their physical and mental health.

The severity of grief is greater among young widows who have had a short span of married life and thus have the burden of looking after very young children. This results in immense emotional and psychological stress, affecting their general status in the family and society and in turn intensifying their social problems.

In the following paragraphs an attempt has been made to study the socio-economic and psychological problems of widows, both working and non-working. At the outset a brief analysis is made about their socio-economic background. This is followed by a detailed discussion of their actual problems.

While 52% of the working widows are below the age of 40 years, 48% of them are above 41 years.

Among the non-working a vast majority of the respondents (89%) are above 41 years and only 11% of the respondents are below the age of 40 years. It is significant to note that of the 89% who are above 41 years 78% of the respondents are above 51 years of age. In general the working widows are younger in age than non-working widows. This may be due to their widowhood at a relatively young age and their consequent earning capacity. Probably they have got jobs on compassionate grounds, on the death of their husbands. The unemployed status of older widows may be due to their old age and that their children could be given the jobs in place of their fathers.

Type of Marriage. The majority of the working respondents had undergone arranged marriages within their castes (92%) and only 8% had had an inter-caste marriage. While 95% of them had undergone a socio-religious marriage only 5% had a registered marriage.

Barring one respondent the rest of the marriages of non-working widows, have been arranged traditional marriages. None of them reported having undergone a registered marriage.

It is significant to note that there are a few working respondents who have had intercaste and registered marriages. This may be due to their greater avenues for outside exposure.

Number of Children in the Households. 11% of the households of working widows are childless as compared to 8% of the non-working widows. Households were categorised on the basis of number of children that each of them had. It was found that most of these families did not have more than 2 children and very few households have more than 4 children.

Sex-wise analysis of the children indicates that in working widows households the number of male children is comparatively smaller than that of female children (62% male, 71% female).

Among the non-working group the number of male and female children is almost equal 64% male and 68% female. In general most of the households of both working and non-working widows belong to the small family size.

Place of Birth and Migration. As regards the place of birth, it is seen that the majority of them were born in urban areas (74%) and 26% were born in rural areas. But a vast majority of them reported urban upbringing (89%).

Analysis of the place of birth or state shows that 87% were born within Karnataka and 13% have migrated from other parts of the country. These being mainly Tamilnadu, Andhra Pradesh and Delhi.

Migration data reveals that of the 87% who were born in Karnataka 66% of them are from Bangalore city itself and only 34% have migrated from different parts of state.

Among non-working widows although the majority of them were born in urban areas (79%) a significant proportion (21%) were born in rural areas. 89% of the respondents lived for the most part of their lives in urban areas and therefore have an urban upbringing. While 95% of the respondents are from Karnataka state only 5% have migrated from other states like Tamilnadu, Andhra Pradesh and Madhya Pradesh.

Migration pattern reveals that of the 95% who were born in Karnatka 69% are from Bangalore city and 31% have migrated from different parts of the state.

Intra and inter migration of the respondents from rural areas and other urban areas to Bangalore city may be due to the educational and employment opportunities and marriage.

Religion and caste. Religion-wise analysis shows that 82% of the working respondents are Hindus 10% are Muslims and 8% are Christians. Among the Hindus, Brahmins form the predominent caste (31%), followed by Marathi with a propotion of 19%. Vokkaliga, Naidu, Reddy, Mudaliar form 11% and Scheduled caste 8%, Lingayats 3% and Gowda 2% form the the rest of the population. 6% of the repondents belong to either Nayakaru Konkini or Shetty caste and the rest 2% did not disclose their caste.

Among the non-working widows 95% of them are Hindus, 3% Christians and 2% are Muslims.

Among the non-working widows Brahmins again form the predominant group (74%) followed by Vokkaliga Naidu Reddy Mudaliar 11%, Gowda 5% Lingayat and Marathi 2% each. One respondent (2%) belongs to Ganiga caste.

In general a greater number of Christian respondents are found among working than non-working widows. This may be due to the lesser degree of restrictions imposed on Christian women in seeking employment.

TABLE W 1.

Distribution of Working and Non-Working Widows by place of birth and place Lived for most part.

Place of birth	*Working widows*		*Non-working widows*		*Lived for the most part of life*	*Working widows*		*Non-Working widows*	
	Total	*%*	*Total*	*%*		*Total*	*%*	*Total*	*%*
Rural	16	26	13	21	Rural	7	11	7	11
Urban	42	74	49	79	Urban	55	89	55	88
Total	62	100	62	100	Total	62	100		

TABLE W.2

Caste-wise Distribution of Working and Non-Working Widows

	Working Widows		*Non-Working Widows*	
	Total	%	*Total*	%
Brahmin	19	31	46	74
Lingayat	2	3	1	2
Vokkaliga, Naidu Reddy, Mudaliar	7	11	7	11
Scheduled caste	5	8	—	—
Gowda	1	2	3	5
Marathi	12	19	1	2
Roman Catholic	4	6	2	3
Protestant	1	2	—	—
Sheik, Sunni, Syeda	6	10	1	2
Not willing to disclose	1	2	—	—
Others	4	6	1	2
	62	100	62	100

For working widows :
Others : 2 Nayakaru
1 Konkani
1 Shetty

For Non-working widows
Others : 1 Ganiga

Educational qualifications of the respondents. An analysis of the educational qualifications of the respondents shows that a greater number of working widows are better educated than the non-working widows. 24% of the working widows have primary education as compared to 45% of the non-working widows. 36% of the working widows have had high school education as against only 16% of the non-working widows and 19% of the working widows are either graduates and or post-graduates as compared to only 5% among the non-working.

TABLE W.3

Educational Qualification of Working and Non-working Widows

Sl. No.	*Educational Qualification*	*Working widows* *Table*	*%*	*Non-working widows* *Table*	*%*
1.	Illiterate	4	6	9	14
2.	Literate without formal education	6	10	11	18
3.	Lower primary (1 to 4th) standard	—	—	9	18
4.	Upper primary (5 to 7th) standard	15	24	19	31
5.	High school education (8 to 10th) standard	22	36	10	16
6.	Inter—P.U.C.	3	5	1	2
7.	Graduate	5	8	3	5
8.	Post-Graduate	7	11	—	—
9.	Technical/professional	—	—	—	—
10.	Others	—	—	—	—
	Total	62	100	62	100

A higher proportion of illiterates was found among non-working widows 32% than working widows 16%.

Thus around 60% of the working widows have high school education and above as against only 47% among non-working widows.

The higher proportion of non-working widows belonging to the relatively older age group and possessing less or nil education may be responsible for their unemployed status.

Occupation and monthly income and number of years of service of the working widows 35% of the respondents who are matriculates are employed as operators in a private factory or firm and 18% of the respondents with less or no education are employed as either ayahs, peons or attenders and 5% as bathi rollers.

Respondents with graduate or post graduate education are mainly employed as clerical staff, (21%) salaried officials (2%) or teachers (19%).

TABLE W.4

Occupation of Working Widows

Sl. No.	*Present Occupation*	*Total*	%
1.	Teacher	12	19
2.	Doctor/Engineer	—	—
3.	Nurse	—	—
4.	Salaried Official	1	2
5.	Clerical Staff	13	21
6.	Ayah/Peon/Attendent	11	18
7.	Pvt. Firm/operator in factory	22	35
8.	Bathi Roller/Tailor	3	5
9.	Others	—	—
	Total	62	100

Data pertaining to the number of years of service shows that the majority of the respondents (51%) have less than 10 years of service while 49% reported experience between 11 to

26 years and more. Of the 51% who have less than 10 years of experience, almost 32% of them have been working between 6 to 10 years.

An analysis of the income of the respondents reveals that more than half of them are earning less than Rs 500 per month (53%). This is largely because a vast majority of the respondents are employed in the private sector where the salaries are generally low. Further they are either engaged in semi-skilled or unskilled labour.

TABLE W. 5

Monthly Income of Working Widows

Sl. No.	*Monthly Income*	*Table*	%
1.	Retired	—	—
2.	Nil Income	—	—
3.	Rs. 1 to 300	14	23
4.	Rs. 301 to 500	19	30
5.	Rs. 501 to 1000	13	21
6.	Rs. 1001 to 2000	14	23
7.	Rs. 2001 to 2500	2	3
8.	Rs. 2501 and above	—	—
	Total	62	100

21% of the respondents are earning between Rs 501 to Rs 1000 per month 23% of them are earning between Rs 1001 to Rs 2000 per month. Only 3% are earning above Rs 2001 per month (26%).

Respondents earning more than Rs. 1000 per month are those who have acquired comparatively higher levels of education and are employed as officials and have put in many years of service.

Type of family. 87% of the working widows are from nuclear families as compared to 77% of the non-working widows. Thus a greater number of non-working widows belong to the joint family than working widows. This may be due to their economic dependence. However, the high proportion of non-working widows living in nuclear families may be because of the combined factors of their belonging to the older age group and therefore having children who are gainfully employed.

Family background of working and non-working widows. The socio-economic factors of education, occupation and income have been taken into consideration when studying family background. An analysis of the educational qualifications of the working respondents' fathers show that the majority are matriculates (40%). 13% of them have either graduate/post graduate or technical qualifications, while 24% are illiterates, 13% are primary educated. Most of them seem to have been employed as salaried non-officials in low paying jobs (34%) and 27% as agricultural workers, coolies, vendors, etc.

Thus more than half of them (57%) are drawing an income of less than Rs. 300 per month. Those who earn between Rs 75 to Rs. 1000 per month are those who are salaried officials or business men.

The educational background of the non-working widows presents a contrasting picture to that of working widows. The majority of the respondents' fathers are educated between 8th to 1(th standard (31%), 33% of them are illiterates or literates without formal education. Around 14% are those educated who are in the graduate/post graduate or professional levels.

In view of their low educational qualification many of them (26%) are employed as vendors, agricultural workers, coolies etc. The next highest proportion is that of those employed as teachers, (19%) and salaried non-officials (13%).

Due to their low educational and occupational status as high as 42% of the respondents' fathers earn an income of less than Rs 300 per month. But those employed as teachers and officials earn more than Rs 751 per month.

Thus in general it is observed that at the higher levels the educational, occupational and income status of the fath ers o the working and non-working widows is almost the same. Butf at the lower levels a higher proportion of fathers of non-working widows have received less or no education and are involved in unskilled labour, and therefore have less income than working widows' fathers.

As regards the educational qualifications of the working and non-working respondents' mothers it is seen that the majority of them are either illiterates or literates without formal education, 60% and 63% respectively, and are mainly housewives 95%, 79% respectively. The comparatively low percentage of housewives in non-working widows' households is due to the lack of information for 14% of the sample.

The influence of the educational background of the family on the respondents' education has been further analysed with the help of educational index[1].

Educational index of parental family. On the basis of the index it it seen that the majority of households fall under the highly educated group households 53%, 24% under moderately educated and 21% under low educated group.

The educational index of the parents' family of non-working widows show that 44% of them come under low educated group followed by an almost equal proportion in moderately or highly educated households (22% and 24%) respectively. While in working widows' households information is not available for 2%, in non-working households the percentage is 10.

In conclusion it can be said that although the parents of the working widows are moderately educated they seem to have encourged their children to receive higher education. Perhaps the early marriage of the working respondents might have prevented them from taking up higher education, while the other younger members of the respondents' family might have availed the same opportunity and consequently got better educated. This explains the reason for the high educational index in these families.

In contrast the low educational background of the parents of non-working widows and their consequent low incomes

1. The index has been explained in the previous chapter on p. 30.

might have been responsible for the low educational index in these families. However, it is encouraging to note that 46% are moderate and highly educated households indicating the upward mobility in these households.

Educational index of the husbands' family. Educational index of the husbands' families of working widows shows that the majority of the households belong to the low educated group households (45%). About 29% of the households either belong to the moderately educated or highly educated group. Information is not available in 26% of the households.

The majority of the households among non-working widows' husbands' families come under the low educated group (42%) with 45% belonging to moderately and highly educated group. Information is not available in 13% of the households.

It is seen that working widows have married into families who fall in the low educational category, when compared to themselves on the index. The non-working widows have married into families of almost their own levels.

Educational index of the family in which the respondents are currently residing : The educational index of the members of the families in which the respondents reside currently shows that the largest proportion of the households of working widows belong to the low educated group (49%). 32% belong to the highly educated group, 19% to the moderately educated households.

In the non-working widows' households, 93% belong to the highly educated group while 24% and 13% respectively to the low and moderately educated households.

In conclusion it is observed that while the educational index of the parents' families of working widows is high that of their husbands' families and the ones they are currently living in is low.

This may be due to the fact that most of the working widows being young are staying with their school-going children (86%). Since most of the children are still in the process of acquiring education the reason for the educational index of these families being low is obvious.

For non-working widows it is observed that the shift has been from low educated households in parents' or husbands' families to highly educated in the current families. Being of an older age group with probably educated and employed children it is not surprising to have a high percentage in the high education category.

Financial status of the parental families and families in which respondents are currently residing.

Proverty line in the parental family. The method for categorising the families by income as those below and above the poverty line has been explained earlier, page 31 Chapter 3. It is seen that the majority of the parents of the working widows are below the proverty line 77% and hence may be considered poor. Only 16% of the households are above the proverty line and information is not available in 7% of the households.

It is significant to note that information pertaining to the financial status of the parents of non-working widows is not available in 39% of the households. Of the remaining 42% are below the proverty line where as only 19% are above the proverty line. In view of the low education, occupation and income of the parents of the non-working widows being low it is quite possibl e that a higher percentage of non-working widows are below the poverty line than working widows.

As regards the financial status of the respondents in the households they are currently living in indicates, a significant number of households are below the poverty line (77%) and only 23% are above the poverty line.

The current financial status of non-working widows indicates that the majority of them are below the poverty lines (68%) of non working widows 32% as compared to 23% of the working widows are above the proverty line. This might be due to the earning capacity of the children of non-working widows.

Since the per-capita income of the family is dependent on the number of members in the households, an analysis of the size of the family from both the parents' side as well as in the families in which the respondents are residing at present has been made.

A comparison of the size of the family of working widows indicates that around 40% of the parents' families belong to medium size households and another 39% to small size households. In view of their poverty and the average size of their families comprising of about 6 members it is not surprising that the per capita income of these families is low.

For non-working widows the majority of the households comprise of 1 to 4 members 62%. The small family size of the households might be one of the reasons for their better standard of living. However this proportion might be slightly over estimated as information is not available for 20% of the households.

As regards the size of the families in which the respondents are currently living it is observed that for working widows 56% of the families have 1 to 4 members while 37% have 5 to 8 members while among non-working widows 52% and 43% respectively belong to the small and medium size families.

In general among working widows there has been an increase in the small families when the family size is compared between parental and current families. For non-working widows the increase has been from small to moderate size families. However the better standard of living in non-working widows households may be due to the following reasons :

(i) The current families of non-working widows though medium sized enjoy a high standard of living as they have grown up children possessing higher levels of education and employed in high paying jobs, bringing in more income as against working widows who in the presence of very young children and the absence of earning members apart from themselves are unable to have a high standard of living.

(ii) Again the working widows have joined the labour force lately, mostly out of necessity after the demise of their husbands. Being less educated and occupied in low paying jobs in private and unrecognised sectors they have a low standard of living.

Assets. As earlier explained (p. 34 Chapter 3) the possession of assets is another criteria for judging the socio-economic status of the families.

A comparison of the value of the assets possessed by the working widows while residing with their parents, their husband's family and their current families shows that the majority of them belong to the low asset group households (*i.e.* nil or assets less than 15) 81%, 75% and 72% respectively.

An analysis of the value of the assets that the households of non-working widows possess from the parent's side, husband's household's side and of those in which they are currently living shows that 71%, 58% and 32% respectively belong to the nil or low asset group households.

In conclusion it can be said that while there is no significant difference in the possession of assets among the working widow's parental, husband and current households the difference is negligible in their husband's and current families. Thus they basically belong to the low asset group.

In the case of non-working widows it is observed that there is a definite shift from low asset possession in parental households to either medium or high asset possession in husband's and current households. Thus they seem to be economically well off and therefore in a position to aquire assests.

Source and amount of income before widowhood and the present source of income. An analysis of the source and amount of income before widowhood reveals that most of them are financially handicapped at the death of their husbands. While 70% of working widows were wholly dependent on their husband's income 4% were dependent on their parent's (as their husbands were unemployed) for livelihood. 26% of the respondents however were employed before widowhood.

Before the death of their husbands non-working widows were either dependent on their husband or children 98% and parents 2%.

A comparison of the amount of income before widowhood among working and non-working respondents shows that while 73% of the households of working respondents earned below Rs. 1000 the proportion of non-working respondents was 50%. This difference in amount may be due to the contribution of an income by children, or because the husband put in many years of service. While among the working respondents children have never contributed to the family income ; and the husbands have died without service accumulation.

Further, the low income of working respondents might be responsible for the respondent having sought employment even before widowhood 26%.

As regards the present source of income it is seen that the majority 56% of the respondents belonging to the working category have joined the work force after the death of their husbands and are therefore solely dependent on their own income for their livelihood for the maintenance of their families unlike non-working widows where the major sources of income are that of their children, husband's pension and a combination of these two sources.

From the above it is seen that nearly 1/3rd of the non-working widow's households have more than one source of income as against 1/10th of working widow's households. The financial condition of non-working widows is therefore better.

Under such circumstances it is not surprising that these widows do not find it difficult to manage their families 61%. Those who have said that they are facing financial problems 39% are mainly being helped either by their children, parents or relatives.

73% of the working widows find it difficult to make both ends meet financially. Respondents getting an additional income from children often complained of their married sons not contributing regularly towards their maintenance.

Also the parents found it difficult financially to help them continuously in view of their own commitments to other younger children in the family.

Facing immense financial problems the respondents were asked as to how they overcame them. The working widows basically resorted to taking loans 31% while the non-working widows reduced their expenses 25%. 34% and 21% respectively of working and non-working widows seek the help of either parents, relatives or friends.

Of those who have taken loans to meet their financial needs, among working widows 53% of them have taken loans ranging between Rs. 1000 to Rs. 5000. The purpose for which loans are taken is either to meet domestic expenditure, to celebrate the marriage or the religious initiation of their children. The place of work, co-operative society, Housing Board, Bank, etc., are the main sources of the loans. A few of them do not pay any interest as they have taken the loan either from friends or relatives. The rest of them pay with an interest ranging between 2% to 8% per month and repay the loans in monthly instalments. Under such strenuous financial conditions it is natural that the majority 53% of working widows reported no savings and only 47% reported saving.

Non-working widows having not resorted to taking loans and as high as 65% of them have reported savings. Only 5% of them have taken loans. They have done so far meeting domestic expenses. They have sought the help of friends and relatives and therefore do not pay any interest.

The financial burden of maintaining the family single-handed seems to have fallen entirely on them. After the death of their husbands the problem of educating and bringing up children is their sole responsibility.

The fact that non-working widows are economically better placed does not mean that they have not faced financial problems earlier. The sample chosen for the study is such that a significant number of them belong to the older age group. However, at the time of widowhood they too would have undergone financial stress as their children would have still been in the education stream. Their own incapacity to earn an income and limited social exposure might have put them under duress. Having always had the support of their husbands, the sudden death of the husband, apart from affecting the financial situation, might have been responsible for increased emotional problems.

The following paragraphs are a detailed discussion of the age at marriage, number of years of married life, particulars pertaining to the cause of the husband's death of the working and non-working widows. 75% of the working widows were married before the age of 20 years as compared to 91% of the non-working widows. Duration of married life indicates that 53% of the working widows lived with their husbands for a period of less than 10 years while 29% lived with their husbands between 16 to 25 years.

In the case of non-working widows 54% of the respondents have had a long married life, i.e., between 26 to 45 years. 10% of them have had more than 46 years of married life.

The age profile of the respondents reveals that working respondents belong to the younger age group when compared to non working respondents. Thus while a majority of working respondents were widowed early, i.e., between the ages of 21 to 35 years, the non-working respondents were widowed at a relatively older age of 46 to 51 years. 53% of the working and 20% of the non-working widows have lost their husbands within the last 10 years.

TABLE W. 6

Age at Widowhood of Working and Non-working Widows

Sl. No.	*Age*	*Working widows* *Total*	*%*	*Non-working widows* *Total*	*%*
1.	Below 15 years	2	3	2	3
2.	16 to 20 years	4	6	2	3
3.	21 to 25 years	10	16	3	5
4.	26 to 30 years	15	24	4	6
5.	31 to 35 years	14	23	5	8
6.	36 to 40 years	9	15	4	6
7.	41 to 45 years	3	5	5	8
8.	46 to 50 years	3	5	12	10
9.	51 & above years	2	3	25	41
	Total	62	100	62	100

An observation of the above discussion reveals that early marriage is a common feature among all the respondents. Unlike non-working widows who have enjoyed long years of married life working widows seemed to have had a short period of married life and have widowed at a very young age.

Since the non-working respondents lost their husbands at a much older age than working widows the problems faced by them might not have been of the same intensity as that of the working widows.

Dowry. An analysis of the details about the payment of dowry during marriage reveals that 85% of the working respondents have not paid dowry while 15% of them paid dowry. Those who have paid have mainly done so in terms of cash (36%) in kind (11%) and in both cash and kind (33%). Since the dowry paid was not controlled by the respondents they were asked as to whether they received the dowry after the death of their husband. To this question all of them 100% replied that the dowry was not returned to them by their in-laws. Among non-working widows 82% of them did not pay any dowry, while 18% of them paid dowry during their marriage. In a majority of the cases (73%,) dowry was paid in kind like gold ornaments and silver articles while in 27% of the cases dowry included cash in addition to that of kind.

As in the case of working respondents even among non-working respondents none of them received the dowry amount after the death of their husbands.

It is interesting to note that an almost equal proportion of non-working respondents have paid dowry as the working respondents. Among the few who have paid dowry, a comparison of the dowry pattern among the working and non-working respondents indicates little difference between them though a slightly higher percentage of non-working than working respondents have paid dowry. However, both groups do not seem to have had any control on the dowry they had given, nor did they receive that at widowhood. One basic difference is in terms of the form in which dowry was given. While the majority of the working respondents did so in cash the non-working respondents have mainly given it in kind.

Cause of husband's death and source of help at widowhood. Illness (38%) and heart attacks (35%) are the two major reasons for the death of the majority of the working respondents' husbands while accidents (16%), excessive drinking (5%), old age (2%) dog bite (2%) and suicides (2%) are the other causes of death.

The cause of death of the husbands' of non-working respondents indicates that the majority of them have died due to heart attacks (37%) followed by illness (35%) accidents (10%) old age (16%) and excessive drinking (2%).

TABLE W. 7

Cause of Death of the Husbands of Working and Non-working Widows

		Working widows		*Non-working widows*	
Sl. No.	*Reasons*	*Total*	%	*Total*	%
1.	Accident	10	16	6	10
2.	Illness	24	38	22	35
3.	Heart attack	22	35	23	37
4.	Excessive drinking	3	5	1	2
5.	Old age	1	2	10	16
6.	Dog bite	1	2	—	—
7.	Suicide	1	2	—	—
8.	Others	—	—	—	—
	Total	62	100	62	100

The categorisation of these respondents' husbands' deaths into those of preventable and non-preventable deaths indicates that a higher proportion of working respondents' husbands have died of preventable death, i.e., accidents, excessive drinking, suicide, dog bite (25%) than non-working 12%.

Present place of residence. The present place of both working and non-working widows shows that 70% and 80% of them respectively are living with their children.

Source of help. Most of the working widows reported that their parents were of help soon after the death of their husbands (44%). While in 35% of the cases relatives and friends seem to have helped them. It is significant to note that in 6% of the cases the respondents were helped by their parents-in-law and 15% of the widows reported that they received no help at all.

Among non-working respondents their children were the major source of help after the death of the husband (57%). While in 23% of the cases both the parents and parents-in-law helped them and 14% of them were helped either by their relatives or friends. 6% reported that they received no help at all.

The non-working respondents, belonging to the older age groups, reported that their grown up employed children have been the main source of help, while for the young working respondents, parents are the immediate source of help.

Further an inquiry into whether they expected any financial and moral help from their husband's family, to take care of their children and themselves, the majority of both working and non-working widows (84%) do not have any expectations.

The working widows being widowed early in life lack financial support and emotional warmth, which in turn increases their sense of insecurity.

The non-working widows due to their long years of married life were not burdened with the maintenance of the familv or with bringing up children single handed. The major responsibilities towards the children seem to have been completed even before the death of their husbands and hence they may not be suffering socially, economically and psychologically to the same extent as working widows.

(ii) Attitudes

Social Status in the Caste/Community. Society promotes the practice of marrying young girls to older men, yet condemns widows to a state of social ostracism.

An inquiry into the status of widows as experienced and perceived by themselves reveals that 79% of the working widows hold a very low status in society in their caste or community, only 14% opined that they are accorded equal treatment with other married women. 5% reported sympathetic treatment from their caste/community people, while 2% were unable to decide the status accorded to them.

A vast majority of non-working widows, 87%, claim that they have a low status in their caste and community. While 11% of the non-working widows report an equal status with other married women, the remaining 2% of the respondents said that they received sympathetic treatment from their caste/community people.

One significant point to be noted here is that working widows seem to be enjoying a better status in society than non-working widows. This may perhaps be due to their earning capacity and consequent economic independence.

In general widows have a very low status in society. A woman after the death of her husband is considered not only inauspicious but also useless. Society prescribes a set of norms which have to be strictly adhered to by these women, failing which they are ostracised.

The norms specify the wearing of simple, sober and cheap clothing. They are not supposed to adorn themselves with ornaments, wear the sindur, thali, flowers as all these are indicative of a sumangali. (Sumangali's are those women who are married and living with their husbands). Widows of some castes are by tradition disfigured. Their heads are shaved and they are made to lead a life of isolation and religious piety.

Against this background an analysis has been made of the widows, their adherence or non adherence to these norms. With respect to change in the mode of dress at widowhood, 56%

of the working widows have changed the mode of dress while 44% have not changed their mode of dress. Of those who have changed their mode of dress as high as 91% have done so on their own accord. While 9% have submitted themselves to the tradition and for fear of social boycott.

Regarding the non-working respondents' change in the mode of dress at widowhood almost 95% of them have changed, and therefore conformed to tradition. Only 5% of them have not changed. The major reasons for conformity to the general practice are enforced traditional social obligation coupled with the fear of social criticism. More working widows seem to be defying tradition and conventions of society than the non-working widows. Their rebellious attitude may be due to their being relatively young and their exposure to the outside world and need to protect themselves from being identified as single and therefore harassed or sexually exploited.

The following is a discussion on the treatment of widows at the work place and in their families.

Status of widows at the work place and treatment by men colleagues. 58% of the respondents averred that their men colleagues treated them with respect at the place of work. Only 11% complained of subjection to ill or indifferent treatment. The problem does not arise for the remaining 30% of the respondents as they are employed in women's organisations.

An extreme case of exploitation is that of a respondent who reported that her superior officials often tried to take advantage of her helplessness and single status. Working directly under him she was often humiliated when she refused to comply to the requests of her boss who wanted her to accompany him after office hours. In such situations the respondent feels extremely vulnerable.

Status in the family. The treatment meted out to widows by family members, relatives and friends reveals that the majority of the widows, both working (53%) and non-working (61%), averred that their family members treated them sympathetically. 18% and 10% respectively of the working and non-working respondents reported indifferent treatment, 29% each from working and non-working categories however reported good treatment.

Relatives of these respondents mete out symathetic treatment to working and non-working respondents in the proportion of 50% and 40% respectively. It is seen that more non-working respondents are treated indifferently 31% than working respondents 27%. And again a higher proportion of non-working widows report good treatment 29% than working widows 23%. A majority of both the respondents reported that from friends they received either sympathetic (working 44% non-working 35%) or good treatment (working 42% non-working 55%).

In general it is noted that family members treat widows sympathetically. Working widows seem to be treated indifferently to a greater extent than non-working widows. It is surprising to note that the majority of them only get sympathetic or indifferent treatment rather than good-treatment. Relatives seem to be more indifferent than family members. However, this sort of treatment is meted out more to the non-working widows. Friends generally mete out good treatment to widows rather than family members and relatives.

Socio-religious participation of widows. Majority of the working respondents, 44%, do not attend or participate in any of the socio-religious functions. While 21% attend either of the functions. The remaining 35% reported that they attend both the functions. Of the working respondents who attend or participate in either of the functions, i.e., social or religious it is seen that attendance and participation is more in religious functions than social functions. Thus around 77% of them attend religious functions as against 23% who attend social functions.

The reasons given for not attending social functions are either they felt discriminated against or out of place. They even complained of ill-treatment in such functions.

The respondents who altogether avoided attending any of the functions also felt that they were not respected in such functions. Most of them felt ill-at-ease in social gatherings and preferred to be on their own than constantly being pointed at as inauspicious.

Among the non-working widows 47% do not attend both the functions while 39% attend both the functions and only

13% attend either of the functions. 2% of the respondents do not have opportunities to attend functions as they are inmates of a destitute home.

An analysis of the type of functions the non-working respondents participate in reveals that of the 13% who attend either functions all of them attend and participate in religious functions only.

It is observed that whether working or non-working, widows in general do not attend or participate in functions, it being more obvious in social than religious functions. Since they are considered inauspicious, the consequent shunning of their presence and the altogether unhealthy treatment that is doled out to them, makes them stay away from the functions.

The reasons for their non-participation is the lack of respect and good treatment that is meted out to them and the sense of alienation they experience at such places. The other reasons are those of old age, ill-health, etc. A few also disclosed disinterest after the death of their husbands in participating in such functions.

Outings. Responses to the question as to whose company the widows seek when they go on outings like going to movies, picnics, shopping, etc., reveal that the majority of the working widows are accompanied by their children (58%) followed by friends (11%) parents, (8%) relatives, (8%). The remaining 15% shop on their own. With regard to casual outings also children are the first to accompany their mothers (55%) followed by by friends (15%) parents (6%) and relatives (10%). 14% of the respondents go on their own.

With respect to non-working widows its is seen that in the majority of the cases they are accompanined by their children 60%, followed by parents 11%, relatives 6%, friends 2%, and by themselves 8%.

As regards casual outings it is seen that again in a majority of the cases children accompany their mothers (55%) followed by parents (13%) relatives and friends (8%). 10% of the rest of working widows go on their own. The rest 13% of non-working widows do not go out anywhere because of old age or illness.

Thus basically widows seek the company of their children. Next to chiidren, working widows are accompanied by friends; the non-working widows depend on their parents. In general it can be stated that children fill in the vacuum created in the mental, emotional and financial spheres. And again working widows are more on their own than non-working widows.

Decisions in the family. A comparison of the role of both working and non-working widows in their families was made. It is observed that with regard to the education, occupation and marriage of children the maiority of them consult one person or the other 58%. The decisions are made in consultation with parents 23% children 83% relatives 13% for working widows, and for non-working widows, children 48%, parents 5% etc. However a higher proportion of working widows are self reliant and decide by themselves—32% working widows, 8% non-working.

Even with regard to taking decisions affecting the respondents' life, buying or selling important goods in the household, many of the working widows consulted no one 36%. A few consulted parents, relatives, children, brothers, sisters or friends 64%.

Among the non-working widows' families it is seen that children are actively involved in all of the decisions made in the family, either affecting the respondents' life or buying or selling goods in the household 69%, 71%.

Decisions are made on a consultative basis in all matters except education at the initial stages. Since the children belong to an older age group they have a major say in all matters pertaining to the family. Working widows on the other hand have to shoulder the family responsibility. In the absence of other members of the family to discuss with, they more often take decisions independently than non-working widows. However, wherever the scope for consultation is available they seem to be eager to grasp the opportunity.

Socio-psychological problems. Respondents were made to reveal wherein they felt handicapped due to the absence of the head of the household. This evoked several reactions. The instances could be broadly classified as two types, financial and socio-psychological. But they are so interlinked that many could not distinguish the difference between them.

Most of the working widows complained of lack of finance, as their major problem. Education of children in general and marriage of female children in particular being their primary concern, 62%. They are in a continuous state of worry as they are unable even to meet their everyday problems. Financial handicap has led to immense psychologicai problems, which has in turn affected inter-personal relations. Thus 15% of the respondents feel unconfident in the absence of the moral support of their husbands. The remaining 20% felt the absence of the husbands when they lacked friendship, emotional warmth at times of distress and support in taking decisions pertaining to the children. Only 3% of the respondents did not feel handicapped because of the absence of their husbands in the family.

Though non-working widows have lost their husbands at a relatively later age than working widows they too cited various instances where the absence of the head of the household (husband) was felt.

The majority of them felt handicapped while taking decisions regarding the education of their children and the marriage of their children, especially that of daughters, 50%, while 26% missed the friendship, emotional warmth and moral support provided by their husbands at times of distress.

The rest 17% reported that they felt handicapped because of their old age and ill-health. Only 6% did not feel handicapped.

In conclusion, it can be said that whether working or non-working, widows strongly feel the absence of the support of their husbands. Their handicap centres around taking decisions about the education, occupation and marriage of their children. This is further accentuated by their weak financial position.

The next major area of deprivation of the husband is on the emotional front. Lack of a companion, his friendship and support is felt to a great extent by the respondents. While this probably is the sole important deprivation they face, the immediate physical problems of that of their children and their future often gets focussed, thereby by suppressing their emotional needs.

In view of the various problems faced by these groups of respondents it is not surprising to note that the majority of them feel lonely, insecure, deserted or frustrated.

The problems that the widows face can be categorised under three headings :

1. The problem of being single.
2. The problem of looking after/bringing up children.
3. The problem from the point of view of status in society.

1. Problem from the point of view of being single. Being single : an almost equal proportion of the working and non-working respondents (42% and 40%) felt the financial stress of maintaining the family alone without the support of family members. Others felt lonely due to lack of companionship and emotionally they were dejected and depressed due to lack of help and support from family members and often did not have the courage to face life alone. 18% of the respondents felt insecure and uncertain about the future. Childless respondents among them were even more apprehensive about their future as they had none to support them even in old age.

A majority of the non-working widows, being of an older age group, reported ill-health, old age, loneliness and lack of mental stability as their main problem (63%). Residing with their children the difference in their outlook, attitudes and values is largely responsible for the indifference that is meted out to them. This generation gap has often resulted in the older widows feeling extremely lonely and isolated. 19% of the respondents reported that irregular financial help from their children led to economic insecurities in maintaining themselves. 13% of the respondents felt uncertain about their future and 5% suffered from emotional and psychological problems like frustration, desertion and emotional insecurity.

2. Problems with Respect to Children. Marriage of children, daughters in particular, and education of children, especially that of sons, seem to be the major problems faced by working widows (63%). With respect to their daughters they are without help in seeking suitable grooms and are unable to accumulate and pay dowry for them. With respect to their sons the high cost of education and the consequent difficulty in raising money to invest in education seems to be their main problem.

Bringing up small children and the difficulty faced in disciplining sons, seemed to be the next major problems of 10% of the widows. Deprived of the love and affection of their fathers it becomes the responsibility of the mothers to play the dual role of both parents to their children. For another 10% of widows the problems are in the form of ill-treatment by sons and daughters-in-law. Desertion by children, maintaining the married daughters and sons-in-law due to the unemployed status of the sons-in-law, and maintaining the widowed daughter-in-law. Only 6% of them reported that they did not face any problem and the remaining 11% are childless. Similarly the non-working widows also complain that performing the marriage of their daughters and educating their sons are their main problems (40%). It may be noted here that although the non-working widows are financially better placed than working widows, yet most of them reported problems pertaining to the marriage of their children. This may be due to high dowry requirements that must be met. Perhaps it is possible to conclude from this that since most of them are old, they are incapable of moving about in search of suitable grooms for their daughters or taking the entire responsibility of performing the marriage. Further they may also be unable to satisfy the unreasonable dowry demands of the bridegroom's families.

Ill-treatment and indifferent treatment and difference of opinion with married sons and their spouses seemed be the next major problem confronting these women. They complained of daughters-in-laws not making necessary adjustments and thereby creating misunderstandings in the family. Often the daughters-in-law did not want them to stay in the house. The constant friction in the family and the unhappy home environment caused them to feel 'unwanted'. Some even reported problems like maintaining the unemployed/mentally unsound children, deserted daughters and their children.

The remaining 11% reported no problems with regard to children, either because they are childless or their children are not alive. 23% of the non-working widows do not have any problems with respect to their chiidren.

3. Problems from the point of view of status in society. Society, according to the working respondents, offers them no sympathy, security, status or position. They are constantly humiliated, harassed and sexually exploited. Others averred that they were degraded and made to feel inferior because of their single status. A few also complained that men often took them to be promiscuous. Men often tried to fill in the emotional vacuum that exists in their lives and then exploit them financially by demanding money at regular intervals. Respondents, though aware of their own vulnerability to such emotional involvements, often found it difficult to be totally uninvolved 73%.

The remaining 27% of the respondents get physically depressed and felt a sense of acute personal loss and a sense of rejection because of the loss of their husbands and hence complain of lack of position and respect in society.

The non-working widows also opine that society does not accord them a place in society. They complain of the lack of position in society in general and among younger members of the family in particular. The indifferent atttitude of the society pained them.

In general the problems of widows are different from those of spinsters in that they have to deal with the bringing up of children. Their perceived status in society is depressing. They are subjected to much humiliation and harassment in society and constant exploitation by family members and by their children. In addition to these, working widows are also exposed to exploitation and sexual victimisation at the work-place.

Leisure time activities. An analysis of the leisure time activities of the working widows shows that 81% of them spend their time in reading. Most of them engage themselves in reading magazines or novels. 5% indulged in literary activities like writing novels, poems or articles. While 8% visit temples or attend discourses, another 6% reported tailoring, handicrafts and knitting as the main leisure time activity.

The burden of maintaining and running the family and working both inside and outside the home perhaps provides them with very little time for themselves.

Reading is the main activity of non-working widows. However, unlike working widows who read novels or magazines they read religious texts. Visiting temples, attending religious discourses are the other main leisure time activities. They together form 76% of the respondents. 11% of the respondents have no leisure time activity for either of the following reasons; they are too aged; ill-health; 8% reported doing odd jobs in the house and looking after grand children. The remaining 5% indulge in teaching music, tailoring and dairying.

TABLE W. 8

Leisure Time Activities

		Working Widows		*Non-working Widows*	
Sl. No.	*Activities*	*Total*	*%*	*Total*	*%*
1.	Reading	50	81	—	—
2.	Writing novels/ poems, articles for magazines	3	5	—	—
3.	Attending discourses, visiting temples	5	8	47	76
	Reading religious books	4	6	—	—
4.	Tailoring, handicrafts knitting				
5.	Old age, sickness	—	—	7	11
6.	Does some odd jobs	—	—	1	2
7.	Looking after grand children	—	—	4	6
8.	Music /Tailoring	—	—	2	3
9.	Looking after dairy	—	—	1	2
10.	Match making	—	—	—	—
	TOTAL	62	100	62	100

The attitudes of working and non-working respondents towards widow remarriage. An analysis of the attitude towards widow remarriage indicates that only 18% of working widows as opposed to 32% of the non-working widows have a totally positive attitude towards widow remarriage: A corollarly to this a higher proportion of working widows, (47%) have a totally negative attitude as compared to that of non-working widows (36%).

An almost equal percentage of working respondents and non-working (35%) and (3.%) respectively feel that a widow should remarry only if she is young and childless.

From the above it is surprising to note that though non-working widows come from relatively traditional homes and have been brought up with a conventional outlook yet they advocate widow remarriage. Perhaps the long years of married life they themselves enjoyed would have been responsible for the realisation that a woman requires the protection and support of a man.

The negative attitude of working respondents however may be due to the presence of very young children and their own commitments and responsibilities towards them. Further they might anticipate more problems by remarrying as they have already been exposed to their own vulnerability at the work place.

Instances of widow remarriage in the family was unknown in the majority of both the working and non-working widows' families (85% and 84%).

About considering remarriage for themselves a vast majority (i.e. 94% of the working widows, 97% of non-working widows) of them averred that they will not remarry even if they come across a suitable match 6% from the working group and 3% from non-working group are prepared to consider remarriage in the event of their meeting the right person.

Most of the working widows anticipated problems from remarriage and therefore were reluctant to take the step since they have children. They fear that they may be ill-treated by their step-fathers (55%).

TABLE W. 9

Opinion About Widow Remarriage

Sl. No.	Remarriage	Workings Widows Total	Workings Widows %	Non-Working Widows Total	Non-Working Widows %
1.	Positive attitude only if widow young and childless.	22	35	20	32
2.	Negative attitude.	29	47	22	36
3.	Positive attitude.	11	18	20	32
	Total	62	100	62	100

Children being their only solace and source of happiness most of them seem to have their welfare and well-being as their main aim, and to reach that end they are willing to make any number of sacrifices.

19% of the respondents feel that they are too old to marry, while 11% said that their conscience does not permit them to remarry. The rest 8% cited the disapproval of society and objections of their parents. Among non-working, the majority of respondents are too old to remarry 19%. While 13% have the welfare of their children in mind. The rest 5% reported various reasons like fear of rejection by society.

It is interesting to note that among both working and non-working windows the reason for not remarrying is external, like the family and society will disapprove of it, and their own responsibilities towards their children, etc.

It is also noted that a higher proportion of non-working widows advocate remarriage than those who would actually consider it for themselves, if an occasion arose. The consistancy in attitude and action seems to be more among working widows than among non-working widows. This may be due to their being practical in view of a society which does not advocate remarriage.

Future Plans. In view of their single status it was deemed necessary to have an insight into what plans they have made for themselves. The majority of them seem to have no particular plans for themselves. They want to continue in their current jobs (68%). Their main aim in life is directed towards the maintaining of their family and looking after the welfare of their children. 19% of them seem to be bound by a strong obligation to their children. They want to educate, conduct the marriage of the children and see them settled in life. Only 6% want to remarry and another 7% want to improve their prospects by better jobs.

As regards non-working respondents 50% of them have no plans in particular. They state that they want to lead a peaceful life.

24% of them plan to conduct the marriage of their children and see them well settled. 18% expressed the desire to be economically independent. They want to secure a job or start a business. While 6% want to go on a piligrimage, the remaining 2% want to settle abroad.

From the above it can be concluded that the majority of the older non-working widows, having fulfilled their responsibility towards their children, look forward to a peaceful life. These widows also exhibit an inclination to religion.

Financial problems and indifferent treatment by older children of the non-working widows is the motivating factor behind some wanting to be economically independent even in their old age.

Thus there is a marked contrast in the future plans of working and non-working widows. Being young and burdened with heavy responsibilities, financial and moral, working women seem to have made more concrete plans for themselves.

Measures Suggested by the Respondents for the Protection of Widows. Respondents were asked what measures they would suggest for the protection of widowed women. The majority of the working widows (41%) were unable to give any suggestion while 36% suggested that government and voluntary organisations should open homes for the widowed women on the lines of the 'Homes for the Aged'.

TABLE W.10 a

Measures Suggested for the Protection of Working Widows

Sl. No.	*Measures*	*Total*	%
1.	Government and voluntary organisations can open homes for aged or Ashrams to help widowed women.	22	36
2.	Old age pension or annual monetary help to be provided by government to all needy widowed women.	11	18
3.	Does not know/cannot answer.	26	41
4.	Financial help by the company in which the deceased worked while in service.	2	3
5.	No measures can help : only kith & kin should help.	1	2
6.	Preference for employment to single women, capable and willing to work.	—	—
7.	To impart vocational skills to the uneducated widowed women to enable them to lead an independent life.	—	—
	Total	62	100

18% suggested that either old age pensions or annual monetary help be provided by the government to all needy widowed women. Thus help could be given to all those having an income of less than Rs. 3,600 per year. 3% suggested that regular financial help be provided by the companies in which their deceased husbands worked while in service. The rest 2% were sceptical and felt that government or organisations would not be able to provide help to widowed women and their kith and kin should help them.

Among the non-working group the majority of the respondents suggested that the government should give pensions or

TABLE W. 10 b

Measures Suggested for the Protection of Widows (Non-Working)

Sl. No.	*Measures*	*Total*	*%*
1.	Government can increase pension or give financial help annually to all needy women, old age homes can be opened.	38	62
2.	Financial help by the company in which the deceaseed worked.	2	3
3.	Cannot answer/Don't know.	16	26
4.	Voluntary organisations/Ashrams can give shelter to destitute widowed women.	2	3
5.	Preference in employment opportunities and vocational skills to uneducated widowed women by government.	4	6
	Total	62	100

annual financial help to all needy women. They also suggested that on the lines of old age homes, homes for the widowed single women be opened (62%). 26% of the respondents could not suggest any measures while 3% of the non-working widows whose husbands were in private companies suggested that financial help be given by the companies in which the respondents' husbands worked. 6% stated that preference in employment opportunities and vocational skills to be given to uneducated women by government.

Conclusion. The discussion of the problems and plight of widows highlights the emotional vacuum that exists in them, the financial upheavals they suffer and the general apathy that is meted out to them. In view of their personal sufferings it is not surprising that they turn to government and voluntary organisations to give relief to them by way of opening homes for their protection.

Adoption. Childless respondents were asked whether they would like to adopt a child so as to provide themselves with moral support and a companion in life, particularly during old age.

Of the 11% of working widows and the 8% of non-working widows who were childless, barring one respondent who desired adoption, the rest were all against it. The reason for not wanting to adopt children revealed that 50% of them reported disinterest, while 33% considered it an additional financial burden. The remaining 17% are at present looking after their nieces and nephews and hence do not wish to entangle themselves in legal adoption procedures.

The reasons of the non-working widows revealed that 75% of them felt that it would be an additional financial and moral responsibility, while 25% reported their husbands were against adoption and even after their demise they were unwilling to go against their husband's will.

Asked about the problems faced by the respondents who wanted to adopt a child both working and non-working revealed that their own parents were their main obstacle. Convincing them was their major problem.

(iii) Case Studies of Working and Non-Working Widows

Introduction. A detailed insight into the problems of widows has been provided in the form of case studies of both working and non-working widows. Thus while each case is unique it is also representative of the many who have the misfortune to be a widow, especially in our Indian society.

Working Widows --Case Study No. 1

Lakshmi, a 48 year old virgin widow, is employed as a school teacher in a private school on a salary of Rs 400 per month. Belonging to a highly conservative brahmin family, and being the only daughter of her parents they wanted to get her married as early as possible to relieve themselves of the responsibility of their only female child. Thus Lakshmi was married when she was hardly 11 years old by the elders in the family to a boy belonging to a respectable brahmin family who was a final year graduate student.

Lakshmi has two older brothers who are educated and employed and well settled in life. Lakshmi, however, could not pursue her education. She was detained at home to prepare herself to be a good customary housewife. She was not sent to her husband's house for two reasons. Firstly, she had not come of age and secondly her husband, still a student, had to complete his education and also secure a job.

But fate seems to have had different plans for Lakshmi. Even after 4 years of marriage Lakshmi's husband could not get through his graduate examination inspite of repeated attempts. Depressed he committed suicide.

Lakshmi's parents were heart broken and grieved much for their daughter. Young and innocent Lakshmi was not in a position to understand the gravity of the situation. But her parents with much understanding and patience were able to disclose to her, her exact status as that as a widow. She was encouraged to continue her education. Although she was a brahmin her parents did not feel the need to disfigure her as most other widows and she was looked after well by them.

In view of the need to be economically independent Lakshmi took up a professional course. She completed her degree in education. After the death of her parents she sought shelter with her brother who by then had been married for some time.

She was looked after well, but soon things went wrong. Her sister-in-law began to till treat her for being a burden on their family, unable to tolerate the insults, Lakshmi decided to be independent and therefore started looking for a job. Inspite of of being trained she was unable to secure a job. With no other alternative she was forced to accept a job in a private school, for a meagre salary of Rs 400 per month.

Though relieved of being a burden to her brother's family, Lakshmi was not happy at her job. Over burdened with a lot of responsibilities, coupled with long hours of work and little facilities she found herself tired both physically and mentally.

At home she was forced to do all the household chores but was not given proper treatment by any of the family members. She was not allowed to participate in any of the family functions as they considered her inauspicious and treated her like an outcaste. None of them showed any sympathy or understanding of her problems.

Lakshmi often felt depressed, lonely and apathetic towards the whole of society. She had none with whom to confide her feelings. She went on to say that she retained her sanity only because of her job which provided her some relief from her worries.

Widowed for over 37 years Lakshmi fears that her early widowhood is the punishment for sins committed in her previous life.

She says that as a single women she had to encounter a lot of problems in life. Asked why she did not marry, Lakshmi said her orthodox parents were entirely against it. After several years she did contemplate marriage but she lacked the courage to confide her desire to any body for fear of being ridiculed and shunned by her family members and relatives.

An enquiry into the plans she has made for the future reveals that she visualises nothing but darkness. She wants to retain her same job until retirement and then plans to use her savings to go on a piligrimage in order to redeem herself from her past sins.

Working Widows—Case Study No. 2

Latha, a 32 year old young widow, is tall slim with attractive features. She is extremely good looking. She comes from a large, rich family of four brothers and four sisters. Her father was an artist who earned his livelihood by selling his own paintings. He was a great lover of fine arts and cultivated the same interest in his children.

Though not very educated Latha showed a great love for dance. She was constantly encouraged by her parents to be a good dancer. Latha staged many performances and has earned a lot of money.

Though her father had a steady income to maintain his family he had inherited ancestral property which belonged to him to provide a luxurious life to his children. Pampered by her brothers and sisters in her parental home Latha grew up with a highly sheltered and protective background, unexposed to the outside world. Her first experience of insecurity was when she lost her mother when she was 12 years old. According to her for the first time she felt "a sense of terrible loss." She was looked after well by her father. At the age of 16 years Latha fell in love with a young handsome Bengali boy who incidentally was her father's friend's son. They got married inspite of much parental opposition.

Latha enjoyed a happy harmonious married life for 10 long years with her husband. Her husband being highly educated and well employed was earning a handsome salary. Latha therefore continued to live in luxury even after her marriage. She gave birth to a daughter after 3 years of married life.

All the problems started for Latha when her husband died of a heart attack all of a sudden.

Having always been provided with a secure life, Latha found it hard to adjust herself to being a widow. The shock and the personal loss which she felt kept her depressed for days. She refused to accept the reality and according, to her she was on the verge of turning insane. It was through the help rendered by family members that she was able to gain the requisite emotional balance.

Her brothers and sisters being married and having their own responsibilities did not come forward to help her. Further her father was too old to help his daughter in any way. Latha for the first time felt she was all alone in this world and in the absence of moral support and an income she had to sell all the property she possessed. It is at this time that she missed her husband's companionship and mental and financial support. She was forced to seek a job to maintain herself and her daughter. She managed to secure a job with the help of her friends and is currently living independently with her daughter.

Nor being accustomed to working outside the home, Latha feels that it is a curse for single women to work outside the home. Young and good looking without a male protection Latha is constantly exposed to unwanted male attention.

She went to the extent of reporting that her boss, 'a much married man' himself, on several occasions had invited her to pay visits with him to some coffee estates. Having intuitively realised his motives she refused his offer to take her out. She has been often threatened with loss of her job. Her continuous refusal to accede to his wish and her expressing her anxiety to her colleagues has infuriated him and resulted in her being ultimately transferred from the department. Currently she is working in a different department.

Even in the present department she is not happy. At the time of interview several comments were overheard all in reference to her beauty, her being single and about her fidelity Not able to withstand such comments, Latha burst into tears. The agony of earning for her livelihood besides being treated as a sex object greatly humiliated her.

She received no help, support or protection from any of her family members. She maintains her daughter and herself on the salary that she earns and therefore she finds it extremely difficult to make both ends meet financially. Her economic pressures are magnified by the fact that she desires to provide her college - going daughter with medical/or engineering education.

She longs for a companion with whom she can confide her her problems especially when she feels utterly confused. Her daughter is too young for Latha either to confide in or discuss problems with. Outsiders/neighbours often look at them with suspicion because they live alone.

Latha has become intensely religious after her husband's death. She visits the temple and prays to God regularly. By this means she has been able to gain peace of mind and stability. Latha has not changed her mode of dress even after the death of her husband. She continues to dress as a married women because that had been the desire of her late husband.

Asked about remarriage, Latha says that she had the benefit of a rich, fulfilling married life with her late husband and as such her memories can never be wiped out by another man in this life.

Her future plans include providing professional education to her daughter and getting her married and seeing her well settled in life.

Non-working Widows—Case Study No. 1

Savithramma is a 65 year old widow who belongs to a conservative family. She has two daughters. She has been educated up to the 7 th standard. She was married at the age of 18 years to a boy within the same caste. Her husband was a graduate and was employed as a school teacher. She had led a happy life till she lost her husband due to heart attack. She was widowed at the age of 60 years.

Though being a brahmin, widowed late in life, Savithramma was not disfigured nor allowed to shave her head by her own family members. She abstains from decorating herself and wears only simple and sober clothes.

Having had both her daughters married, at widowhood she has been living with her younger daughter and son-in law. She has been looked after well by them. Financially she does not face any problem as her late husband left her financially sound. Psychologically she feels very lonely in life. Accustomed to her husband's company and support she misses him at every point in life.

Being quite aged she has not been keeping good health and she rarely goes out of the house. She abstains from attending any social function. She feels that widows are treated with disrespect. Further, of late being aged and leading a happy married life she was often drawn to the forefront and made to play an important role in all social activities, and now all of a sudden she is pushed to the background. This sudden switch in importance, she has not been able to accept and therefore finds it more embarrassing to attend them.

Savithramma is very orthodox and is totally against the idea of widow remarriage. She plans to visit various places in the future.

Non-working Widows—Case Study No. 2

Ratna is a 30 year old childless widow from a lower middle class family. Being an orphan she has always been supported by her relatives. She was married to a petty shop owner by her relatives. A year ago he died of a heart attack.

Ratna's life has been full of agony after her husband's death. She has been forced by her relatives to disfigure herself and prevented from decorating herself Being young, Ratha finds it a great torture to lead a widowed life.

At the death of her husband her relatives have taken possession of the shop which her husband owned on the pretext of helping her manage the shop and make business. Slowly she has been totally alienated.

At home, she is made to do all the household chores, the cooking, cleaning, etc. Besides she has to look after the children in the family, do petty marketing all alone. She is not given scope to go out nor enjoy herself or wear good clothes.

Her basic needs are also not met. Often she is the last person to eat at home, and the left overs are mainly given to her. She feels that even the maids are treated better than her. She does not get the moral protection or support from her relatives. Instead she is constantly abused for being a burden.

As a result of this she feels lonely and insecure and dejected in life. Ill-treated without means for her livelihood Ratna feels utterly dejected in life. She wants to adopt a child to overcome the sense of loneliness but fears that she may not be able to support the child.

Constantly forced to do the physical work Ratna has not been keeping good health and she cannot afford to go to a doctor due to her financial problems. Like a typical Hindu widow she is "Condemned to a life of drudgery, Ratha spends her days in utter sorrow".

Asked about her future plans, she says that she wants to join a destitute home where atleast she can be independent and free from physical and mental tortue.

Conclusions. The case studies of the widows presented here depict the low status that is meted out to widows. On the one hand they are considered inauspicious and therefore shunned and ill-treated; on the other hand they are constantly exploited both physically and emotionally.

5

Profile of Divorced and Separated Women

(i) Demographic Details

The concept of divorce is a relatively novel phenomenon in Indian society. Indissolubility of marriage no longer holds good. Traditional values are being replaced and society is undergoing a radical transformation.[1]

The disappearance of the joint family which provided security to women as well as to other members of the family, both emotional and social, encouraged the values of sacrifice, respect for age and authority. Discussing the concept of the traditional Hindu marriage and family Kapadia writes, "Marriage was a social duty towards the family and community and there was little idea of individual interest. The social background provided by the authoritarian joint family and caste with its domination in all spheres of life afforded no scope for the recognition of any personal factor, individual interests and aspirations, in the relations between husband and wife." (Kapadia 1958 p. 169)

Marriage was not meant mainly for individual gratification, individual interests and aspirations, but was rather a social duty towards the family and community, where little happiness was expected in marriage. There was hardly any question of recognising any marriage as unhappy and the problem of marital adjustment therefore never came to the forefront.

1. *Divorced Hindu Women*. Rama Mehta (Desai 1957 pp. 224).

"Good marital adjustment was possible within the frame work of a traditional Hindu family. The large joint family supplied the husband and wife with contemporaries, in age and sex, with whom they could get 'companionship satisfaction'. This may be one reason for their relatively good adjustment for they were not wholly dependent on each other for deep affection or companionship". (Ross 1961 p. 155)

Another reason was due to the roles, status and obligations of husband and wife being markedly specified so as not to permit any conflicts between them[2]. (Goode 1965 p. 72)

"The process of industrialisation and urbanisation and secularisation has brought about the socio-psychological changes in the attitudes and values of the people of this country especially among the urban population. The attitudes of educated women have considerably changed particularly with regard to marriage and their own status."[3]

More and more women consider self respect and development of personality as necessary goals of life. The two fold pillars of Hindu society viz: Sacramental marriage and joint family are weakening.

Though the modern family gives independence to a women she is no longer able to cope with the stress and strain of marriage in view of the dual role which she has to play, both as a mother and housewife and that of a working woman.

Economically independent women, as earning members, expect some sort of respectful position in the family. When they are denied this respect at home by their husbands, or/and in-laws and are treated as either money-making machines or passive partners, the suppressed personality of these women revolts and seeds of conflict are planted resulting in separation or divorce.[4]

The divorced/separated women are looked upon with contempt and as such do not hold a respectable position in society.

2. Quoted in *Marriage and working women in India*—Promilla Kapur 1970 p. 8.
3. *Marriage and working women in India*—Promilla Kapur 1970 pp. 11.
4. *Ibid.*

Under the circumstances it is important to investigate the problems of such women.

In the following paragraphs an attempt has been made to study the socio-economic background and problems of divorced and separated women.

(i) Demographic Details

The age profile reveals that the majority of the working divorced/separated respondents (74%) are below 40 years while 26% are above 41 years.

Among the non-working a vast majority of them are below 40 years (88%) and only 12% are above 41 years.

In general working respondents are older than the non-working respondents. However, it is evident that whether working or non-working their marriages have concluded in divorce/separation at a relatively young age.

Type of Marriage. An analysis of the type of marriage of the working respondents reveals that 82% of the respondents have undergone arranged marriages within the caste and 18% have had inter-caste or inter-religious marriages.

All the respondents who have married outside their own caste have chosen their life partners and in the case of those where marriages were arranged, barring one respondent who chose her own partner, the parents have been responsible for the selection of life partners.

While 86% of them have undergone socio-religious marriages, 14% of them have had registered marriages

Among the non-working as high as 94% of the respondents have reported arranged marriages within the caste and only 6% (4 respondents) reported either inter-caste/or inter-religious marriages. Barring those who have had registered marriages (5%) all of them have had socio-religious marriages 5%.

It is observed that a higher proportion of working respondents have married outside their own caste than non-working respondents. The greater exposure of working respondents to the outside world might have provided them with more opportunities to interact with people and therefore enabled them to choose their own life partners.

Number of Children. An analysis of the number of children in the households reveals that the majority of them either have one or two children. (66% working 58% non-working). None of the households from both working and non-working have more than 3 children. This again may be because most of them had a short span of married life.

As high as 34% of the working respondents do not have any children, as against 42% of the non-working respondents.

The age profile and the number of years they have remained married also reveals that they have had a short married life. Perhaps the maladjustments of the couples and the strained inter-personal relationships and consequent separation may be one of the reasons.

Place of Birth and Migration. The place of birth of the majority of the working respondents reveals that they are from urban areas (92%). While 8% are from rural areas most of the respondents have reported an urban upbringing (95%).

It is further seen that 87% of the respondents are domiciles of Karnataka and the remaining 13% have migrated from other states like Kerala, Tamil Nadu, Andhra Pradesh and Maharashtra.

Migration data reveals that of the 87% who belong to Karnataka 77% are from Bangalore city itself and the rest 23% have intra-migrated from districts like Hassan, Tumkur, etc.

Among the non-working, 73% are born in urban areas and a significant proportion of the respondents are rural born (27%). Inspite of the place of birth being rural areas, the data indicates that the majority of them (89%) have had an urban upbringing.

While 95% of the respondents are natives of Karnataka 5% of them are migrants from either Tamilnadu or Maharashtra.

Even among this group intra-migration is very uncommon. Of the 95% who are natives of Karnataka, 64% are from Bangalore city and 36% have migrated from different parts within the state.

Thus it is seen that of the two groups more non-working respondents have a rural background than working respondents. However, the place of birth of the majority of both working and non-working respondents is Bangalore city itself. Inter-state

TABLE D. 1

Distribution of Working and Non-working Divorced/Separated Women

1. Place by birth (Rural and Urban)

Place of Birth			
		Working D/S	*Non-working D/S*
Sl. No.	*Place of birth*	*Total & %*	*Total & %*
1.	Rural	5—8%	17—27%
2.	Urban	57—92%	45—73%
	Total	62—100	62—100

2. States

State of Birth			
		Working D/S	*Non-working D/S*
Sl. No.	*State of Birth*	*Total & %*	*Total & %*
1.	Karnataka	54—87%	59—95%
2.	Kerala	1—2	— —
3.	Tamil Nadu	5—8	2— 3
4.	Andhra Pradesh	1—2	— —
5.	Maharashtra	1—2	1— 2
6.	Madhya Pradesh	— —	— —
7.	Uttar Pradesh	— —	— —
	Total	62—100	62—100

migration is higher among non-working than working respondents.

Religion and Caste. Religion-wise analysis shows among working respondents 84% are Hindus and 11% Christians and 5% are Muslims.

The caste-wise breakup indicates that among Hindus, Brahmins form the predominant group (41%) followed by Gowda 15%, Vokkaliga Naidu, Reddy, Mudaliar form 10% and Lingayats 7%, Marathas and S.C. form 3% each and 6% other castes. Among the non-working 88% of them are Hindus, 10% are Christians and 2% are Muslims.

Among the Hindus, Brahmins again form the predominent group (44%) followed by Gowda 19%, Vokkaliga, Naidu,

TABLE D. 2

Caste-wise Distribution of Working & Non-working Divorced/Separated Women

	Working		*Non-working*	
Caste	*Total*	*%*	*Total*	*%*
Brahmin	25	41%	27	44%
Vokkaliga, Naidu Reddy, Mudaliars	6	10%	4	6%
Lingayats	4	6%	2	3%
Maratha	2	3%	2	3%
Scheduled caste	2	3%	3	5%
Gowda	9	15%	12	19%
Catholic	5	8%	4	6%
Protestant	3	5%	2	3%
S.S.S.	2	3%	1	2%
N.W. destitute	—	—	—	—
Others	4	6%	5	8%
Total	62	100%	62	99%

Reddy, Mudaliar form 6% and Lingayats and Maratis form 3% each, 5% belong to Scheduled caste and the remaining 8% belong to various other castes. One significant point to be noted here is that among both working and non-working groups, the incidence of divorce/separation is found among the most traditional community, i.e., Brahmins. This may be due to the purposive nature of the sample selected and it may not be representative of their proportion in the population.

Educational Qualification of the Respondents. An analysis of the educational qualifications of the working and non-working respondents shows that 50% of the working respondents have either graduate, post graduate, technical or professional education as compared to only 23% of the non-working respondents. It is surprising that inspite of high educational qualifications a significant proportion are not employed, perhaps the lack of job availability may be one of the reasons.

Again 32% of the working respondents have had school education (Matriculation and below) as compared to 63% of the non-working divorced/separated respondents. 8% and 6% of the working and non-working respondents respectively have had intermediate education and the remaining 10% of the working respondents are either illiterates or literates without formal education as against 8% of the non-working respondents.

In general a higher proportion of working respondents are better educated than non-working respondents. However, it is of significance to note that the majority of non-working divorced/separated respondents have high school education (42%).

Occupation, number of years of service and income. In view of the high educational qualifications it is seen that most of the respondents are placed in relatively good jobs. The majority of the respondents are employed as operators in factories 32%, followed by 26% as clerks, 19% as teachers 13% as professional or salaried officials. Only 9% are employed in unskilled occupations as ayahs, peons, attendants, etc.

An analysis of the number of years of service indicates that most of them (45%) have accumulated an experience of less than 5 years while 26% report a work experience of 6 to 10 years and 29% of more than 11 years.

TABLE D.3

Educational Qualification of Divorced/Separated Women

		Working		*Non-working*	
Sl. No.	*Educational Qualification*	*Total*	*%*	*Total*	*%*
1	Illiterate	3	5	1	2
2	Literate without formal education	3	5	4	6
3	Lower Primary (1 to 4th standard)	4	6	5	8
4	Upper Primary (5 to 7th standard)	3	5	8	13
5	High school education (8 to 10th standard)	13	21	26	42
6	Inter, P.U.C.	5	8	4	6
7	Graduate	15	24	13	21
8	Post Graduate	14	23	1	2
9	Technical/Professional	2	3	—	—
	Total	62	100	62	100

Though a high proportion of respondents have a small number of years of work experience their monthly income is between Rs 1001 to 2501 per month. They form 31% of the sample of working respondents. While 26% earn between Rs. 501 to 1000 per month, 43% of them are earning below Rs. 500 per month.

Perhaps it is possible to conclude from this these respondents being well educated are engaged in occupations paying higher incomes.

Type of family. The type of family to which the respondents belong reveals that the majority of those belonging to the working group (89%) are from nuclear families while the rest

(11%) are residing in charitable organisations run by government, or in hostels.

Among the non-working group 72% are from nuclear families 5% from joint families, as high as 21% are from state owned reception centres for destitute women, i e., (Abhaya Ashram) only 2% are at present residing in hostels.

It is interesting to note that though single a large number of working divorcees or separated women live in a nuclear family. Even among the non-working respondents the joint family system is not prevalent to a significant extent. Perhaps these women do not receive the support of the joint family because of their unconventional dissolution of marriage.

Again more non-working divorced/separated women reside in destitute homes as they do not have economic security to be independent.

Family background of the respondents. The educational background of the parents reveals that the majority of the working respondents' fathers are graduates, post graduates, professional (41%). 26% of them are educated between 1st to 10th std. 19% of the respondents' fathers are either illiterates or literates without formal education. In the rest (14%) of the cases the details on education are not available. As a consequence of their high education around 40% are engaged in better jobs of a professional, executive and mana erial nature. As such, 33% of them earn a salary of Rs. 1000 to 2000 and above per month. 19% of the respondents' fathers are skilled workers, and as such 11% earn a monthly income between Rs. 501 and Rs. 1000. 21% of them who are semi skilled or unskilled workers, earn less than Rs. 500 per month (36%) In the remaining 20% of the cases the occupations and incomes of the fathers, are not recorded.

The educational qualifications of the fathers of the non-working respondents reveals that the majority of them have had school education 35%. 24% of them have had either graduate, post graduate or professional/technical education. 31% are illiterates and the rest, 10%, of the respondents' fathers have had non-formal education.

An occupation-wise analysis shows that 21% of them are employed in professional, managerial and executive occupations, and basically earn a monthly income of Rs. 1001 to Rs. 2000 and above, 23% of those engaged in skilled work earn between Rs. 501 to Rs. 1000. The rest 42% are employed in either semi-skilled or unskilled jobs like vendors, cooly, agriculture workers, etc. Their earnings are generally below Rs. 500 per month (45%). In 14% of the cases occupations and incomes are not recorded.

Thus, in general it is observed that fathers of the working respondents are more educated and have higher paying jobs in comparison with those of non-working respondents who have basically held positions in either low paying, semi or unskilled labour.

More than 65% of the respondents' mothers both working and non-working are either illiterates, literates without formal education or primary educated. Even among those who are educated almost all have received only high school education. Thus more than 85% of them are mainly occupied as housewives. Those employed were engaged mainly in unskilled and semi-skilled work and therefore their monthly earnings did not exceed Rs. 300

In general the working group have a comparatively better background than non-working respondents. In view of the differential educational status of the parents of the working and non-working it will be of interest to evaluate the education of the other members in the family. The educational index, developed for the purpose has been used to compare and analyse the educational status of the respondents' parents, parents' family, husbands' family and the current family.

Educational index of the parents' family. 61% of the households of the working respondents' parents' families belong to the high education group and 24% to the moderately educated group, only 13% are from low educated group. Information is not available in the remaining 2% of the households.

In contrast, the index for the non-working respondents indicates that 48% of the households belong to the highly educated group and 28% to the moderately educated group and 21% of them belong to the low educational group households. Information is not available in 3% of the households.

Thus a higher proportion of respondents in the non-working

group belong to the low or medium educated households (nearly 50%) than in the working group 37%.

Educational index of the husband's family. Similarly the majority of the working respondents' husbands' families are highly educated as is observed from the fact that 46% of them belong to the highly educated group households while 15% belong to the moderately educated households. 31% of the households are from the low education group. Information pertaining to the education of the members is not available in 8% of the households.

The index for the non-working respondents indicates that while 31% belong to highly educated group 34% and 27% belong to the moderately and low educated group of households respectively.

In general while 61% of the non-working respondents' husbands' families fall in the moderately and low educated households, the proportion is 46% for the working respondents. It is significant to note, however, that a higher percentage of working respondents have married into families having low educational status than non-working respondents.

Educational index of the respondents' current family. The Educational status of the members of the family where the working respondent is currently residing shows that the majority of them belong to the low education group household (58%) whereas 29% belong to the highly educated group, and 13% to the moderately educated group household.

In the 'currently living' families of non-working respondents 47% of the households belong to the low educated group. While 34% belong to the highly educated group 19% belong to the moderately educated group.

The reasons for the generally low educational status both in the working and non-working respondents' families may be summarised thus:-

Firstly the majority of the respondents have either no children or very young children who are still in school, consequently their educational index is low.

Secondly as high as 27% and 31% of the working and non-working respondents are living independently in hostels, destitute homes or reception centres. In such cases the education is bound to be low as only the respondents' education is taken into account, which incidentially is not high. This has already been mentioned earlier.

In conclusion the mobility pattern that emerges from an analysis of the educational index of the parents', husbands' and current families of the respondents reveals a downward trend. The data reveals a definite increase in the proportion of respondents belonging to the low educated group of households when a comparison of the 3 types of families is made in the said order of parents', husbands' and current households. This downward shift from highly educated to low educated households is surprisingly more among working than non-working respondents.

Financial Status of the parental families and the families in which the respondents are currently residing. Education being highly inter-co-related the income as a variable has been used to study the economic standard in terms of the poverty line of the respondents' families, both that of their parents and their own.

The economic standard of the husbands' families have not been accounted for, as the majority of the respondents were unwilling to impart such information as they were divorced or separated.

An analysis of the poverty line in parents' families of working respondents shows 42% of them are above the poverty line and 48% are below the poverty line. Information is not available for 10% of the households.

Among non-working respondents 72% of the parents' family are below the poverty line and 17% are above the poverty line. Information is not available in 11% of the households.

The economic standard of the family is the function of the size composition of the households. 45% of the working respondents' families, and 53% of the non-working respondents' being either medium or large sized comprising of 5 to 9 or more members it is not surprising that 48% or 72% of them are poor. Further the low education of the parents and family members of non-working respondents and the consequent low income may be another factor contributory to their poverty.

Poverty line in the families in which the respondents are residing at present. 50% of the households of the working respondents are below the poverty line, while 42% of the households are above the poverty line. Information is not available in 8% of the households.

Among the non-working respondents 66% of the households are below the poverty line and 11% are above the poverty line. Information is not available in the remaining 23% of the households.

Since the per capita income is the function of the size of the family an analysis of the size of the families shows that 71% and 69% respondents of the working and non-working respondents' households are small size, comprising of 1 to 4 members.

The small size of both working and non-working respondents' families may be the main factor responsible for those above the poverty line. However only 11% of the non-working respondents' families are above the poverty line as against 42% of the working respondents' families. Again this may be due to the non-earning capacity of the respondents who are not working.

An interesting observation is that there is no difference in the economic standard of the parents' families and the current families of working respondents. Among non-working respondents there is a decrease in the proportion of those who are below the poverty line when a comparison of their parents and current families is made.

Assets. The socio-economic status of the families is further evaluated by the value of the assets that they possess. The method used for the evaluation of the family assets has already been explained.

The highest percentage of households of working respondents belong to the middle asset group on the parental side (32%) nil asset group on the husbands' side (39%) and low assets group in their current position (61%). Among non-working respondents the majority of both the parents' (39%) and husbands' (37%) families belong to the low asset group while in their current position they belong to the nil asset group (46%).

In general it is noted that the parents' families of the working respondents were better placed than those of their husbands. But in relation to their husbands' families their current families are slightly better.

TABLE D. 4

Occupation of Working Divorced/Separated Women

Sl No	*Present Occupation*	*Total*	*%*
1	Teacher	12	19
2	Doctor/engineer	2	3
3	Nurse	—	—
4	Salaried official	6	10
5	Clerical staff	16	26
6	Ayah/Peon/Attendant	2	3
7	Pvt firm. Occupation in factory	20	32
8	Bathi roller/Tailor	4	6
9	Other	—	—
	Total	62	100

Two points may be noted here to explain the mobility in family status. Firstly a significant number of respondents here have had a marriage alliance with partners belonging to a lower socio-economic group than that of the parents' family. The differences in the status of their husband's and their own family and the consequent financial constraints faced by them might have resulted in adjustment problems leading to marital conflict and ultimate separation/divorce.

Further, a significant number of working respondents married outside their caste or have undergone love marriages. In such marriages the socio-economic level is not taken into consideration. This may be one of the reasons for the differences and downward mobility from that of parents' to that of husband's family. In case of marriages arranged by parents, failure on the part of parents to secure a suitable match, within the similar socio-economic strata might have forced them to marry off their wards to persons belonging to the lower economic strata.

Secondly, being separated/divorced and being employed they are able to improve their status inspite of being burdened with the responsbility of maintaining the families.

For non-working respondents, the parental and husbands' families belonged to the same level, while the current position is lower. This may be explained by the fact that though non-working respondents have married into families of similar standard as that of their own, after separation or divorce their status has deteriorated on account of their unemployed condition.

TABLE D. 5

Working Divorced/Separated Women

Sl No	*Monthly income*	*Total*	*%*
1	Retired	—	—
2	Nil income	—	—
3	Rs. 1 to 300	19	30
4	Rs. 301 to 500	8	13
5	Rs. 501 to 1000	16	26
6	Rs. 1001 to 2000	16	26
7	Rs. 2001 to 2500	2	3
8	Rs. 2501 and above	1	2
	Total	62	100

The financial condition of the respondents can futher be known from the source and amount of income before divorce/ separation and their present source of income.

Source and Amount of income before Divorce/Separation and Present Source of Income. Before the divorce/separation, in 50% of the respondents' households the husband was the only bread-winner in the family while in 34% of the households the respondents supplemented their husbands' income. In 6% of the households the respondents were the only earning member in the family. The remaining 10% reported various sources of income. From the above it is observed that as high as 50% of the respondents joined the labour force only after their divorce or separation.

As quite a significant proportion of respondents were employed even while they co-habitated with their husbands, the amount of income earned in the majority of the households was relatively high, i.e., between Rs. 1001 to 2501 and above per month. (48%)

In contrast 96% of the non-working respondents were solely dependent on their husband's income for their livelihood and the rest 4% reported nil income because their husbands were pursuing higher education. As such as the amount of income earned in the majority of the cases was between Rs. 500 to Rs. 1000 per month (61%).

Further, an analysis of the present source of income, apart from occupation, reveals that 87% of the working respondents reported no other source of income apart from their own income and only 13% have reported various sources like land, children's income or income from parents, brothers, etc. While for non-working 90% reported no source of income and 10% reported various sources like children's, parents' or income from the person they intended to marry or interest from fixed deposit, etc. Under such circumstances the majority of them reported no savings (97%) and only 3% have some savings.

Among working respondents 61% of the respondents reported savings and only 39% did not report any savings.

An analysis of 'loan taken' indicates that the majority of the working respondents have not taken loan (94%) only 6% reported taking a loan either for domestic expenditure or to purchase a vehicle. The amount of loan taken ranged between Rs. 1000 to Rs. 5000.

The source of loan is either the place of work or friends.

The repayment of loan in all cases is in terms of monthly instalments without interest. Only one respondent reported paying an interest at the rate of 3%.

None of the non-working respondents resorted to taking loans. Since their financial position is strained 89% of them, though willing to accept financial help from their husbands, were not getting any help. Only 6% of the respondents have refused financial help and 5% are at present getting maintenence from their husbands.

In conclusion it can be said that the financial position of the non-working group is not very sound. Though a sizeable number of families are small and are childless, yet their financial position is quite weak. Failure on the part of the husbands to provide for a living after separation, without any help from parents-in-law or parents add to their financial constraints, unlike the working who are able to manage inspite of all these because of their earning capacity.

In conclusion it can be said that the majority of the respondents after separation/divorce from their husbands do not seem to be maintaining the same level of living.

In the following paragraphs the details of the respondents' marital status like age at marriage, number of years of married life and the age at separation or divorce is analysed in detail to examine the relationship between these variables in the light of adjustment problems in marriage and divorce/separation.

Age at Marriage. The majority of the working respondents 72% were married before they attained the age of 25 years. Of them a significant 50% were married before the age of 20 years.

A majority of the respondents, 63%, separated within 5 years of married life while 34% lived with their husbands between 6 to 15 yrs. Only 3% separated after 16 to 25 yrs of married life.

The age at separation of the respondents indicates that 45% of them separated when they were in the age range of 21 to 30 yrs, 31% did so in the 31 to 35 yrs of age. Surprisingly 14% before they attained the age of 20 years and the rest, 10%, after 36 years of age. Thus 58% of the respondents were separated within the last 5 years, 24% between 6 to 10 years ago, 15% between 11 to 25 years ago and the rest, 3%, were divorced about 31 years ago.

TABLE D. 6

Age at Marriage of Divorced/Separated Women

Sl No	*Age at marriage*	*Working* *Total*	*%*	*Non-working* *Total*	*%*
1	10 years and below	—	—	—	—
2	11 to 15 years	9	14	6	10
3	16 to 20 years	16	26	29	46
4	21 to 25 years	20	32	20	32
5	26 to 30 years	9	14	6	10
6	31 years and above	8	13	1	2
	Total	62	100	62	100

As regards the non-working, 88% of the respondents were married before the age of 25 years and of these 56% were married before the age of 20 years. The rest, 12%, were married between the age of 26 to 31 years and above.

Even among the non-working respondents the majority had separated within 5 years of married life, 60%. While 27% lived with their husbands between 6 to 15 years, 10% lived together from 16 to 25 years and 3% had more than 26 yrs of married life.

The age at which they separated reveals that 63% did so between 21 to 30 years, while 14% separated when they were 31 to 35 years. 12% before 20 years and 11% after 36 years and above. Thus most of the respondents separated 5 years ago, 85% Only 9% between 6 to 10 years ago and 6% separated as long as 16 to 31 years ago.

In conclusion, it can be said that the majority of both working and non-working respondents married before 25 years of age. However, a larger proportion of non-working respondents have had an early marriage when compared to working respondents. But both the categories of divorced/separated respondents have separated early in life. However, a higher proportion of non-working respondents have lived with their husbands for a longer period of time. Economic independence of the working group might have given them greater confidence to separate, unlike non-working who were solely dependent on their husbands' income for their livelihood.

The findings of the study is consistent with the findings of other research studies on "Age and marital happiness." To quote, Burgess and Coltrell in a study of 526 marriages found more unhappy marriages among men who married at 22 and women who married under 19 years. Similarly Terman's study of 792 marriages showed unhappy marriage among men who married under 22 and women who married under 20 years.

So also Landis and Landis (1958 p. 131) in his study of approximately one thousand couples also showed more unhappy marriages among men and women who married under 20 years.[1]

The studies mentioned above indicate findings which are similar to the findings of this study. The present study also evinces that a significant propotion of women who married below 20 years had unhappy marriages.

Selection of Marriage Partner. The 'persons responsible for selection of marriage partners' indicates that 74% of the working respondents were married to persons selected by their parents whereas 19% of them made the choice themselves. While in 3% of the cases the married sisters of the respondents made the choice and in another 3% the choice was in joint consultation, with the parents. The consent of the majority of the respondents was however taken into consideration, 8 %. In 18% of the cases it is significant to note that respondents were forced to marry the person selected either by their parents, sister or relatives.

Even among the non-working respondents the choice of marriage partners was basically made by their parents, 81%. One respondent chose in consultation with her parents. In 3%

[1]Quoted in Dr. Promilla Kapur's book

of the cases the relatives chose the marriage partner for the respondents and the remaining 14% chose the marriage partner themselves. Of them, 5% have had love/registered marriages and for the rest (though they made the choice), their marriage was performed in a traditional way after the approval of the parents.

The consent of 87% of the non-working respondents was taken before the marriage, while in 13% of the cases they were forced into marriage.

In conclusion it can be said, although the working group seem to have had a greater decision making role in selecting their marriage partner, quite a significant proportion seem to have been married without their consent. Also it is noted that inspite of better education and economic independence, more working respondents than non-working were forced into marriage by their parents. These respondents seem to have become victims of orthodox and conventional parents whose only concern was to get their daughters married. Lack of consent of the respondent before marriage also seems to be one of the reasons for separation/divorce.

Though a significant number of the non-working respondents were also not consulted before their marriage they seem to have continued to live with their husbands primarily due to their economic dependence, unlike working respondents who were economically independent.

Dowry. Information pertaining to payment of dowry was collected from respondents to see how many respondents had paid dowry and whether they received the dowry after separation/divorce from their husbands

63% of the working respondents had not paid dowry, while 37% reported that they had done so. Of those who had paid, 31% had paid both in cash and kind while the remaining 6% paid either in cash or in kind.

Asked whether they were able to recover the dowry amount after their separation/divorce as high as 91% of the respondents answered in the negative while only 9% reported that they received back the amount. The reasons given in most of the cases was unwillingness on the part of the husband or parents-in-law to give back the amount, 57%. 28% of the respondents had not maintained contact with their spouses. This hindered the possiblity of collecting back the dowry. The remaining 15% of the respondents could not recover the dowry amount as it had been misused by the husband or spent to meet the health demands of the husband.

As regards non-working respondents it was seen that while 53% of the respondents had paid dowry, 47% had not paid dowry. Of those who had paid dowry 44% reported payment both in cash and kind, 9% had paid dowry either in cash or kind.

Even among the non-working majority, 91% of them reported non-receipt of the dowry after separation or divorce from the husband. The reason given in most of the cases was unwillingness on the part of the husband's family to return the dowry amount, 60%. 33% of the respondents did not maintain any contact with their husbands after separation to recover it. In 7% the dowry has been misused by the husband and hence was unrecoverable.

Being employed and earning a regular income it was not surprising that a higher percentage 63% of working respondents had not paid dowry as compared to non-working respondents 47%. Perhaps their earning capacity even before marriage was one of the factors responsible for the non-payment of dowry. Refusal to pay back the amount and misuse of the dowry amount by in-laws and husbands were the main reasons for non-payment among both working and non-working divorced/separated women.

Type of Divorce/Separation. An analysis of the type of divorce/separation reveals that 63% of the respondents were separated, while 24% had applied for legal divorce and the remaining 13% of the working respondents were legally divorced.

Among the non-working it was seen that 50% of the respondents had applied for legal divorce while 47% were separated from their husbands only. 3% of the respondents were legally divorced.

Though more working respondents were legally divorced than non-working respondents a greater number of non-working women were seeking a legal divorce currently than working women. Lack of a job to support themselves and their children and an alternative to make a livelihood might have forced more non-working divorced/separated women to seek legal divorce, through which they could claim maintenance and allowance from their husbands.

Reasons for Divorce or Separation. An analysis of the reasons for divorce or separation reveals that various factors have forced the respondents to separate from their husbands.

The majority of the working respondents 29% averred that ill-treatment by the mother-in-law and husband was the main reason for separation or divorce. The husband and his family members were the main source of marital friction. They expected the respondent to manage the entire household work without any assistance. Dual responsibility of the respondent for earning an income and doing all the household chores often resulted in quarrels and tensions between the spouses in particular, and in the family in general.

Most of the respondents also confessed that the frequent insults, humiliations and continuous harassment for more dowry by their parents-in-law forced them to seek separation/divorce.

This is supported by other studies on "Divorced women" conducted by Rama Mehta, who states that :

"Majority of women found the dominance of their in laws very difficult to accept. In-laws expected unquestioned submissiveness to their will, whereas the educated women did not want to accept authority". Thus indignant treatment, physical cruelty and mental torture made them leave their husbands.

23% of the respondents left their husbands because of their husband's irresponsibility, bad character and failure to contribute towards the family income. 18% separated because of the extra marital affairs indulged in by their husbands Greed for money, forcing the respondent to prostitute in order to make quick money, sexual perversion and impotency of the husbands has made 7% of the respondents seek separation.

Of the remaining 23%, excessive drinking 5%, suspicious nature of the husbands 3%, marriage forced against the respondents will 3%, desertion 3%, information pertaining to the first marriage of the husband 2%, mental unsoundness 2%, acute illness 2%, or childlessness 3%, have been the reasons for separation.

TABLE D. 7

Reasons for Divorce or Separation among Working Respondents

Sl No	*Reasons*	*Total*	*%*
1	Ill-treatment by mother-in-law and husband (harassment for dowry)	18	29
2	Irresponsibility, failure to contribute to family income and bad character of the husband	14	23
3	Extra marital affairs of the husband	11	18
4	Forcing wife to take up prostitution/ sexual perversion/impotent	4	7
5	Excessive Drinking	3	5
6	Suspicious nature	2	3
7	Forced marriage against the respondents will	2	3
8	Desertion, has left for gulf country/ U.S. has not returned	2	3
9	Was already married before	2	3
10	Mentally unsound	1	2
11	Paralysis or illness	1	2
12	Childlessness	2	3
	Total	62	100

To conclude, in the words of Promilla Kapur, "The changes in the life pattern of working women have brought about a definite change in her personality, her attitudes and her behaviour. Her economic self-reliance has made her conscious of her rights and she is intolerant towards social injustice. On the other hand the social attitudes of discrimination against her continue to be more of a rule than exception. It is this gap in the attitude of men and women that creates conflict, confusion and tension in a women's marital and family relationships."[1]

As regards the non-working respondents it is seen that again ill-treatment and harassment both physical and mental by a husband and his family members, especially mother-in-law, is the main cause for separation (28%). 26% separated due to the indulgence of their husbands in extra marital relationships 11%.

TABLE D. 8

Reasons for Divorce/Separation among Non-Working Respondents

Sl No	*Reasons*	*Total*	*%*
1	Ill-treatment or harassment both physical and mental by husband, mother-in-law and family members	17	28
2	Extra marital affair	16	26
3	Harassment for dowry	7	11
4	Irresponsible behaviour and failure to perform his duties as a head of the family	7	11
5	Irresponsible desertion, has not returned	6	10
6	Impotent/homosexual	4	7
7	Incompatability, fights frequently	2	3
8	Forced marriage	1	2
9	Boy mentally unsound	1	2
10	Respondent bore a female child	1	2
	Total	62	100

1. Dr. Promilla Kapur *Femina* June 23rd to 7th July 1985.

reported that they were harassed for more dowry. Irresponsible behaviour of the husband and failure to conform to his duties as the head of the family has resulted in conflicts and tensions terminating in separation/divorce, in 11% of the cases.

The other reasons stated by the rest are : irresponsibility and desertion (10%), impotency and homosexual behaviour of the husband (7%) and incompatibility, frequent fights (3%) forced marriage of the respondent (2%) and unsound mental condition of the husband (2%) and failure to produce a male child 2%.

It is observed that whether working or non-working, conflict and tensions arising from the ill-treatment meted out to them by their husband and his family is the main cause for termination of marriage.

In general the findings and observation of Dr. Promilla Kapur are quite relevant to this study, "The causes for divorce among the middle class is economic Financial constraints tear them apart whereas among the upper class incompatability and infidelity plays an important part. Among the lower class both the reasons operate."

Initiative for Divorce/Separation : An analysis of the data regarding the persons responsible for initiating the divorce or separation reveals that among the working group the initiative was taken by the respondents themselves (60%). In 27% of the cases the respondents' husbands were responsible for the divorce or separation, 9% of them separated due to parents-in-law or parents' initiative. In one case 2% the brother of the respondent took the initiative and in another 2% both the respondent and her husband mutually initiated the divorce or separation.

In contrast among the non-working group the initiative for divorce was taken mostly by the respondents' husbands (37%) followed by respondents themselves 31%, and their parents or parents-in-law 22%. 8% of the respondents jointly with their parents took the initiative for divorce or separation. In one case (2%) the respondent's sister-in-law was responsible for it.

In general it was observed that a greater number of working respondents had taken the initiative for divorce/separation than non-working respondents. Again their economic independence might be one of the factors which had influenced them to take this bold step. But it is interesting to note that more non-working respondents were currently seeking legal divorce in order to claim maintenance from their husbands.

Contact with family of parents-in-law. An almost equal proportion of 86% of the working and 89% of the non-working respondents do not maintain any contact with their in-laws' families.

During the course of the interview a few working respondents reported that their parents-in-law took the initiative of maintaining contact with them. Probably, according to the respondents, their parents-in-law were attracted by the income they earned. They used all techniques of extracting money from them.

An enquiry into the necessity of financial help from parents-in-law reveals that more non-working respondents (43%) expect their parents-in-law to take care of them and their children than working respondents. Being deserted by their husbands and with no alternate avenues of income for their livelihood, it is obvious that the non-working respondents expect the assistance of their parents-in-law.

Custody of Children. As already stated 34% of the working respondents as compared to 42% of the non-working respondents are childless.

Of those with children the majority of both the working and non-working respondents have their custody. (56%) and (46%) respectively.

This is due to the fact that the children are infants thus necessitating their living with their mother. Among the working respondents who do not have custody of the children, parents, parents-in-law (7%) and husband (2%) have custody. One working respondent (2%) has left her child in boarding school.

While among the non-working, husbands (5%), parents-in-law, parents (4%) others, mother or sister of the respondents (2%) have the custody. One respondent 2% reported that though both she and her husband took care of the children alternately, the child lived with her.

An allowance towards maintenance. An analysis of the data on evidence of respondents receiving an allowance towards maintenance from their husbands, reveals an interesting result.

Among the working (98%) and non-working (95%) most of the respondents were not getting a maintenance allowance from their husbands. Only one respondent of the working category and another three (5%) from the non-working category got some financial assistance from their husbands.

The reasons for not claiming maintenance indicate that 34% of the working respondents' husbands have refused to give an allowance. However 28% of the respondents either did not ask for it or could not claim maintenance as they did not know the whereabouts of their husbands

Some of the working respondents said that they did not want to live on the mercy or charity of their husbands.

15% did not maintain any contact with their husbands while in 13% of the cases the husbands had either remarried or kept a mistress. In either case they did not have enough money to give them an allowance.

In the rest, 10%, of the cases the respondents' husbands were unemployed and therefore unable to give maintenance.

An analysis of the reasons among non-working respondents indicates that refusal on the part of the husband to give any financial help was the main reasons (27%). In 25% of the cases the respondents and their husbands had not kept contact with each other, after separation.

Unemployment or remarriage of their husbands had prevented 16% of the respondents from asking them for maintenance.

In 18% of the cases the respondents did not know the whereabouts of their husbands and hence were unable to claim maintenance. Another 14% of the respondents aver that they would rather manage on their own than ask for financial help from their husdands with whom they wish to sever contact.

The following points emerge from the above data :

1. Very few respondents from both the working and non-working groups get an allowance towards maintenance from their husbands.
2. Refusal on the part of the husband is the major reason for not getting maintenance among both the groups.

Economicaly self-sufficient working respondents do not want to take financial help from their husbands, and live on their charity, whereas among non-working respondents, lack of means to maintain themselves has forced more non-working respondents to seek their husband's help and also seek legal divorce in order to claim redress from them in the form of maintenance.

(ii) Attitudes

Social Status of Divorced or Separated Women. The word divorce is a taboo in Indian society. Divorced women are ill-treated, harassed and regarded as aggressive women. Therefore women in society prefer to live in the guise of a happy marriage than seek divorce or separation.

A general analysis of the social status in society of the divorced or separated women as perceived by the respondents themselves shows that 87% each, of both those working and non-working, possess a low-status.

Only 11% of working respondents and 13% of non-working respondents were of the opinion that no such discrimination existed and that they enjoyed the same status as that meted out to other married women. One respondent from the working group could not answer.

The reasons for the low status that most of these respondents hold are the absence of a male as the head of the household and loss of their own identity and lack of respectability in society because of their single status. Most of them said that they are treated as women with no morals. Often they are shunned and regarded as 'aggressive', 'permissive' and social outcastes for deviating from the customs and traditions of the society, thus making it extremely difficult for them to lead a satisfactory social life. This is further supported by Rama Mehta.

"Divorced women were regarded as poor unfortunate women. They were made to feel discarded by family and society as if they were existing on charity. Thus most of them found it difficult to establish a satisfactory social life."

The social status of single women, especially that of divorced/

separated, women is aptly described by Kalarani in her book *Role conflict in working women.*[1]

"Neighours pity widows, but for separated aad divorced women they do not have a good opinion. Women neighbours are always afraid of them. Even their husbands would not allow them to mix with separated or divorced women, as sueh women are not admired in society. Separated and divorced women also feel uncomfortable in the company of the other married women specially those who do not work outside. Such women have fewer guests and visitors". Thus in general the social status of the divorced/separated women is very low.

Status of Divorced/Separated women at the place of work. At the work place divorced/separated women become the focus of gossip and male attention. Often they are looked at by men with lust and treated as permissive and easily available women. One respondent went to the extent of remarking that if she ignored the advances of her boss, he harassed her by either allotting her a heavy work load or threatening to transfer her to some remote area in the state. Unable to reveal this to her colleagues she subjected herself to great mental torture. This has seriously affected her health both physical and mental.

The study showed that married women usually avoided the company of divorced/separated women for fear of being branded as loose women. In general it was impossible for working separated and divorced women to present a picture of respectability which married women so easily got just because they lived with their husbands, without consideration to their happiness.

Status in the family. It is heartening to note that though treated with contempt in society at least the members of the families are giving them good and sympathetic treatment.

77% of the working respondents as against 81% of non-working respondents said that they received good or sympathetic treatment from their family members. 23% of the working respondents and 19% of the non-working respondents were treated indifferently by the members of their families.

[1]*Role conflict in working women* by Kalarani
Chapter: 'A case of widowed/separated/divorced working women'.

The relatives of more than 50% both of working and non-working respondents (57% and 52%) respectively treated them indifferently. Shunned and often avoided by their relatives they are made to feel 'Sinners' who have committed an unpardonable 'Crime', according to Rama Mehta.

"Deserted by kith and kin and ill-treated by caste/community members, the respondents suffered from a great sense of abandonment".

But it is encouraging to note that 37% of working respondents and 40% of the non-working respondents received sympathetic treatment from their relatives.

Most of the respondents confessed that they received mixed treatment from their relatives. On the one hand they were ridiculed, and on the other hand they were also pitied. A few respondents were indifferent about the treatment meted out to them. They were of the opinion that they did not require the sympathy of their relatives as the motive according to them was mostly derogative. (To degrade them).

Only 6% of the working and 8% of the non-working respondents reported good treatment by their relatives. However, in relation to friends the majority of both working and non-working respondents (63% and 55%) reported good treatment.

The following observations emerge from the above discussion :

1. More non-working respondents are given good treatment by their family members than working respondents.
2. Secondly, higher proportion of non-working respondents' relatives are sympathetic towards them than of working respondents.
3. Thirdly, friends seem to be a greater source of support and help than either relatives or family members of respondents, in both the groups.

Deserted by husband without any means to maintain themselves, perhaps non-working single women evoke more sympathy than working women who are economically self-sufficient.

Social Interaction

Attendance and participation in social and religious functions. The divorced or separated women, in view of their single status, often have to face a lot of embarassment in society and in consequence their interaction with other members of the society is often limited. If widows are considered inauspicious, the divorced/separated women are treated with contempt and are regarded as bad omens by orthodox and conservative families. But being 'sumangalies' [1]they are not debarred from participation in such gatherings.

Thus the majority of working respondents 92% are invited to both the social and religious functions by relatives and friends. Only 8% of them (5 respondents) who are staying in Ashramas or reception centres are not invited to such functions as they do not maintain cordial relationships with other relatives or friends.

Among the non-working respondents the majority of them (79%) are invited to both the social and religious functions. While the rest (21%) who are residing in ashram or state owned reception centres do not attend such functions due to absence of contact with relatives and friends.

Regarding attendance among both working and non-working category 45% do not attend either of the functions, 47% of working respondents attend either and 34% non-working respondents attended both or either of the functions.

Of the 47% of the working respondents who attend either functions it is seen that all of them attend and participate in religious functions. Whereas only 26 respondents 20% attend social functions the remaining women 5% do not attend social functions, for fear of social boycott. Most of them confessed that fear of relatives and friends and asking embarassing and personal questions prevented them from attending such functions. Among non-working respondents barring one respondent all attend religious functions, and regarding social func-

[1]A *sumangali* is a married woman whose husband is alive. It is of no importance whether the marriage works or not.

tions of the 84% only 28% attend social functions and 6% do not attend.

The reasons given by the respondents who do not attend any of the functions are in the order of ill-treatment. Fear of social boycott or gossip, feeling of alienation which they experience in such functions and dejection in life, prevent them from attending such functions.

In conclusion it can be said that working respondents are invited to a greater extent than non-working respondents. But it is interesting to note that though no restriction is imposed on their attendance or participation by custom, yet most of these women prefer to avoid them and the unnecessary social exposure and the related embarassment of their marital breakup.

Outings Respondents were asked as to whom they depended on while going out to attend functions. An analysis of the data reveals interesting results.

Majority of working respondents 46% while going out to attend socio-religious functions like marriages, initiation ceremonies, religious meetings and visiting the place of worship depend mainly on their children, followed by parents who form the next source of companionship 31%. 23% of the respondents attend on their own.

While among the non-working respondents it is seen that parents of the respondents 41% form the main persons of companionship followed by sisters 23% and children 18% accompany the respondents. 18% of the respondents however attend on their own.

With regard to shopping or casual outings most of the working respondents again depend mainly on their children (32%) followed by parents (28%). A significant proportion of the respondents 23% go out on their own. The remaining 17% of the respondents depend on either friends or siblings.

While the non-working respondents depend mostly on their parents 63%, followed by children 19%, friends 8%, and sisters 2%. 8% of the respondents go out alone. A point to be noted is that most of the non-working respondents are childless and therefore their dependence on members in the parents' family is greater than in the working group.

For the working respondents however their economic independence and exposure to the outside world might have instilled in them a sense of confidence and consequently would have lessened their feeling of dependence on others.

Decision making. An analysis of the decision making power of the respondents in their households with regard to the education, occupation and marriage of their children shows that decisions are mostly made on a consultative basis. The majority of the working respondents (29%) who have children consult their children themselves about any decision which would affect their lives while 18% of them take independent decisions about their children's future, 11% consult their relatives or friends and 8% their siblings. 34% of the respondents are childless.

Among the non-working respondents the majority of them consult their parents 34% followed by those who independently decide 10%, 9% consult their brothers or sisters and children.

While in the case of 5% of the respondents all the responsibilities regarding their children are at present over, they are well settled at the moment. 42% of the non-working respondents are childless. With regard to buying or selling of goods in the family or taking decisions affecting their own lives while the children play the prominent role for working respondents for non-working respondents parents are the main consultants.

From the above it may be concluded that in the households of working respondents the opinion of the children is of importance in taking decisions while in the non-working respondents' households parents of the respondents are consulted before taking decisions. This is because of their entire dependence on their parents.

Leisure time activities. An analysis of the leisure time activities of the respondents reveals that majority 58% of the working respondents indulge in reading while 23% of them spend their time in tailoring, handicrafts, knitting or learning fine arts like music or dance. 3% of the respondents who are religiously inclined engage themselves in religious activities like reading religious texts and in visiting temples while another 3% involve themselves in creative writing for magazines, journals, etc. The remaining 5% watch movies, 8% of them are engaged in Ashram work for the whole day and therefore do not find time for leisure.

As regards the non-working respondents it is seen that 50% of them indulge in light reading or attend a degree or diploma course. 29% of the respondents spend their leisure in handicrafts, knitting, watching movies, giving tuitions, tailoring or visiting temples.

TABLE D.9

Leisure Time Activities of Working and Non-Working Divorced/Separated Respondents

Sl No	*Leisure time activities*	*Working*		*Non-Working*	
		Total	*%*	*Total*	*%*
1	Reading/attending Degree or Diploma course	36	58	31	50
2	Tailoring, handicrafts, knitting or learning music, tuition	14	23	16	26
3	Visiting temples or attending discourses	2	3	2	3
4	Writing novels and articles for magazines	2	3	—	—
5	Watching movies/rolling bathi	3	5	—	—
6	Ashram's Work	5	8	13	21
	Total	62	100	62	100

However 21% of the destitute women who are staying in Ashrams or reception centres are engaged in the centres' work and hence do not have much leisure.

From the above it is seen that the major leisure time activities of both working and non-working respondents is reading. A large number of non-working respondents seems to be attending some educational course in order to improve their prospects of securing a job.

Problems at work. Working women are the victims of a double exploitation, by the family and society. Being divorced or separated, 29% of the respondents complained that they were treated with contempt and curiosity at the place of work. Often they were subjected to unnecessary questioning with intent to hurt. To quote Kalarani, "Since most of the colleagues were married and living with their husbands they did not want a single woman in their company and most of them were indifferent".

The main problem as revealed by the respondents at the work place is that of being taken advantage of by their male colleagues due to their single status. They are often made to feel that they are women of loose morals and hence unable to lead a happy life. They are doubly at a disadvantage when they worked directly under a male employer or supervisor, who does not hesitate to use his position of authority to harass and sexually exploit them (28%). Kalarani states. "Behaviour of the employer was good where the employer was the lady but in the case of the male supervisor there was some danger. In such cases respondents had to be cautious and alert."

Another 25% of the residents complained not only of harassment at the place of work but also of the job, low wages, long hours of work and primarily of sexual exploitation by the employer or superior. Only 18% of the respondents of whom quite a few were employed in organisations concerned with women's issues complained of no problems at the work place.

Problems at home. The problems these single women face can be grouped under the following headings :

1. Problems from the point of view of children
2. Financial problems
3. Psychological problems
4. Problems in the family and society

50% of the working respondents feel lonely, insecure and

uncertain about the future. Most of them reported that they suffer from tensions and lack peace of mind which in turn has seriously affected their mental health. According to Kalarani, "Almost all the respondents do not have good health. This is due to their worries because all the time consciously or in their subconscious they feel that they are alone, leading a life without husbands".

The next major problem is in terms of finance. They, being the sole earning member of the family, a significant 24% of them reported financial problems. Maintaining day-to-day household expenditure, providing for the education of the children and accumulating the dowry for female children formed their main concerns.

The respondents (14%) also complained of the problems of adjustment with siblings especially those who are married and face no marital disharmony. Their own failure in marriage has been the cause for indifferent treatment and sometimes even ill-treatment by family members. Some respondents reported being deliberately misunderstood on issues of minor concern.

The main worry of childless respondents centred around the problem of loneliness and the probable deprivation of support and help during their old age (12%). However, respondents with many young children were worried about ways and means of bringing up their children single handedly without the support of a husband.

Contrastingly there is a definite shift in the order of the problems enountered by the non-working respondents. The majority of them were faced with financial problems (59%). Without means to support themselves and their children most of them are financially crippled and therefore worry themselves immensely about their day-to-day subsistence. 21% of the respondents who reside in homes for the rehabilitation of destitute women, apart from being faced with the problem of finance, are also subjected to social and psychological problems. Being destitute most of them received no help or support from their own family members or from society. Most of the children of these respondents, (though they are allowed to stay in Ashrams) are the responsibility of their mothers and solely dependent on them. The burden of bringing up the children and providing for their education and marriage seems to be their major worry.

The children who were below 5 years though allowed to stay with their mothers in these homes were not given any special care, nor provided with extra facilities. They were treated as adults and the mother had to feed her children within whatever she got from these homes. Apart from this the respondents were worried about the children above 5 years who were not allowed to stay in destitute homes.

10% of the respondents were concerned about providing dowry for their daughters' marriage. They were apprehensive that their daughters might remain unmarried due to their inability to pay the requisite dowry.

Another 10% of the respondents considered themselves a burden to their parents. This was in consequence of the constant worry of the parents regarding the respondents' future.

In conclusion it can be said that the problems faced by the respondents depended on their education, socio-economic status and the number of children they had. Those possessing little or no education or unemployed and having children were the worst hit.

Psychological problems. Respondents were asked to list the various psychological problems they faced. All the respondents (100% both working and non-working) suffered from a sense of loneliness/insecurity, the cause of which was deep depression and dejection in life.

None of them reported being happy. Separated/divorced by their husbands, plagued by financial problems, constantly harassed by both family members and society, it is not surprising that the majority of the respondents feel insecure. Most of them have neither the will nor the desire to live. To quote Ram Mehta, "The women who undergo divorces suffer a lot of trauma and tensions in life. They need mental rehabilitation and anchor to tide over emotional problems".

Plans of marriage. Responses to the question whether the respondents would like to remarry if an opportunity arose revealed an almost equal porportion of the working and the non-working disagreeing with remarriage (90% or 89% respectively). Only 10% from the working and 11% from the non-working group desired remarriage.

An analysis of the reasons for not considering remarriage as given by the working respondents reveals that 34% of them having suffered the trauma of a bad marriage are reluctant to enter into matrimony for the second time, Ram Mehta states.

"Second marriage was considered as a high risk proposition and many respondents felt that their own experience with marriage had left an indelible memory of suffering. They did not want to enter another close relationship in which the possibility of failure was potentially present."

24% of the respondents reported that as they were disillusioned by marriage, they expected more hassles from a second marriage and they were not interested in even considering remarriage.

The view expressed by the respondents are in accord with that of the study conducted by Ram Mehta on divorced women. He says, "Most women were bitter and having been demoralised and humiliated the divorce came as a relief from tyranny and tension".

18% of the respondents who have children do not want to marry again because of the ill-effect it will have on their children.

Commenting on this Ram Mehta says :-

"Majority of the divorced/or separated women regarded marriage as immoral or unethical proposition. Most of them did not contemplate remarriage mainly due to social circumstances or due to the effect that it will have on children". Since the majority of the respondents look after their children and consider them as their only source of happiness they do not want to spoil the relationship with them".

The rest 10% of the respondents are not willing to remarry because of various other reasons like wanting to have a career, to live independently, waiting for the divorce to be granted or because they are unable to conceive.

It is interesting to note that 14% of the respondents do not want to remarry because they hope for a reconciliation with their husbands. This clearly indicates that these respondents consider their separation as a temporary measure and look forward for a reconciliation with their spouses. This adherence to the traditional value of preferring an unhappy married life to separation or divorce may be due to the trauma they experienced at the hands of society. The reasons as given by non-working respondents reveal that the majority of them are apprehensive of remarriage failure. The main reason is the fear of failure in choosing the partner. Beside most of them say that they are tired of marriage and men (38%).

While 25% of the respondents do not want to remarry because they have children, 15% of them feel that they are too old to remarry. Another 5% want to live independently while the remaining 2% are not able to conceive and therefore do not contemplate remarriage.

Similarly to the working group even among the non-working a significant number of respondents (15%) want to be reconciled with their husbands. The stigma attached to a divorced/separated in the society perhaps makes them opt for reconciliation rather than for a marriage breakup.

To conclude in the words of Ram Mehta, "Even the most educated and liberated feel that from a social angle it is women and children who have to suffer because of divorce. Most men get away at the most by paying a meagre portion of their income and are free to seek fresh pastures. It is the woman who has to start again from scratch."

Respondents, working (10%) non-working (11%) who expressed the desire to remarry were asked whether they have taken any decision about their partners.

Almost all the respondents among both working and non-working (barring one respondent each in both categories) who desire remarriage have not decided about their marriage partner. The other two respondents who had taken the decision, however, were not acquainted with them prior to their first marriage.

Plans for the future. An anaylsis of the plans the respondents have made for the future among the working category reveals that 35% of them have the responsibility for bringing up, educating and getting their children married. All their plans centred around providing for them. 27% of the respondents stated that they had made no particular plans for the future except that they continued to attend to their work in a routine manner.

11% of the respondents want to improve their prospects by

seeking a better job. While 10% of the respondents wish to remarry, 10% desire reconciliation with their husbands. A few of them want to go abroad or take up private tuitions after retirement (5%).

However, one working respondent (2%) who was extremely dejected in life had a nervous break-down during the interview. According to her, she had reached a point where suicide seemed the only solution to her sorrows.

Among the non-working respondents the majority of them (50%) are in search of employment in order to be economically independent. While 16% stated that their goal in life was to educate and get their children married, another 16% reported that they have no plans in particular. 11% of the respondents desire remarriage. Future plans of the remaining 7% of the respondents included reconciliation with their husbands, setting up their homes (5%) and moving out of the destitute homes to live independently (2%).

In conclusion it is observed that most of the respondents' plans for the future are oriented towards the welfare and well-being of their children. The non-working respondents whose major aim is to seek employment is also mainly for the purpose of providing for their children.

Adoption. Childless respondents were asked their opinion on adoption, whether they themselves would like to adopt a child and the reasons for wanting to adopt a child or not.

95% of the working respondents as against 100% of the non-working respondents are against adoption. The reasons given by the majority of both the working and non-working respondents are as follows :

Most of them consider the upbringing of a child an additional responsibility. In view of the financial constraints they face themselves they consider the adopted child more of a liability than an asset. As such they were not interested in adopting a child.

A few think that such children will be ungrateful to them when they learn about their true parentage and therefore sacrifice on their own part for their well-being is not considered a worthwhile cause.

Two of the working respondents take care of there nephews

and therefore do not feel the necessity to adopt a child.

Policy Measures. Respondents were asked to outline the measures to be adopted for the protection of single women during their old age. To this the majority of the working respondents suggested that old age homes should be opened by the government (47%).

36% of them feel that the government should start hostels for such women on subsidised rates, so that they are not a burden to their parents or relatives. A few respondents suggested that a pension on similar lines to an old age pension should be given to single women.

While 6% are of the opinion that religious institutions should give protection to single women, 3% were skeptical

TABLE D.10a

Measures Suggested for the Protection of Single Women by Working Divorced/Separated Women

Sl No	*Measures*	*Total*	*%*
1	Old age homes for the single women by the government	29	47
2	Subsidized hostels for needy women or can be given government pension so that they need not be burden to parents	22	36
3	Religious institutions or Ashrams can give protection to single women	4	6
4	Government cannot do anything, kith and kin should help	2	3
5	Cannot answer/don't know	5	8
	Total	62	100

about the help government can render, therefore they feel that they should depend only on their kith and kin and 8% could not answer.

Non-working women suggested that government should reserve jobs for single women (24%). While 22% of them suggested the opening of homes for single women, 19% felt that voluntary organisations should take up the cause of single women, and plead with the government for annual financial help. Another 19% feel that all single women should be given a pension, on similar lines to old age pension. 9% of the respondents profess the view that single women be vocationally trained so as to improve their opportunities in the labour market. Of the rest 5% could not answer and 2% were skeptical about government help.

TABLE D. 10 b

Measures Suggested for the Protection of Single Women by Non-Working Divorced/Separated Women

Sl No	*Measures*	*Total*	*%*
1	Government can give jobs or reserve jobs for single women	15	24
2	Homes for single women, to be opened by the government on the lines of old age homes	14	22
3	Voluntary organisations can take up the cause with government and plead for annual financial help	12	19
4	Old age pension can be given to single women	12	19
5	Provision of vocational skills to all single women	5	9
6	Don't know/cannot answer	3	5
7	Government cannot do anything only kith and kin should help	1	2
	Total	62	100

In conclusion, it can be said that the measures outlined above by these respondents reveal that according to them a lot can be done for their protection and cause both by the government and voluntary organisations. Co-ordinated efforts on the part of government and voluntary organisations can help to minimise the problems and lessen their financial and psychological problems.

Divorced and separated respondents were asked a series of questions to find out the circumstances under which they feel a woman is justified in initiating a divorce/separation from her husband.

One significant point to be noted here is that 97% of the working respondents feel that a woman may divorce or separate from her husband if she faced problems for which there were no solutions.

Only 3% of the respondents feel that under no circumstances should a woman initiate a divorce or separation from her husband.

An analysis of the circumstances under which divorce or separation could be initiated reveals that 58% of the respondents are in favour if a woman is subjected to physical cruelty, harassed for dowry, or the husband is irresponsible and does not provide for his family.

A few among the above also feel that incompatibility, failure to adjust and build a rapport even after several years of marriage may be a ground for seeking divorce or separation.

26% of the respondents said that the woman should divorce her husband if he is unfaithful to her. The remaining 8% of the respondents reported that impotency, gambling or drinking may be grounds for divorce or separation. (5% of the respondents could not answer).

Even among the non-working respondents the majority of them 51% feel that if husbands and members of his family ill-treat or mentally harass the woman, she is justified in seeking a divorce/separation.

The other circumstances enumerated are in this order: extra marital affairs (19%), harassment for dowry (8%), irresponsible behaviour (4%), impotency, homosexuality, lack of mental compatibility (4%).

Only 3% were firm that a woman should never separate or

take divorce from her husband under any circumstance. (11% of the respondents could not answer).

From the above it is observed that women whether financially independent or not are no longer prepared to live with their husbands, if they are not treated with due respect and consideration. They seem prepared to live alone a 'life of dignity' rather than suffer at the hands of their husbands. Thus, they no longer view a marriage partnership as an indissoluble union under all circumstances.

Awareness regarding legal divorce. Separated/divorced respondents were asked whether they were aware that they could obtain legal divorce from their husbands and the reasons for not undergoing legal divorce.

Among the working, as already mentioned earlier, only 8% of the respondents were legally divorced. Though 93% of the respondents were aware that they could obtain legal divorce only 7% were not aware of it.

Among the non-working group, barring one respondent who is legally divorced, almost all,94% were aware that they could obtain a legal divorce. Only one respondent (3%) was unaware of the relief that the court can sanction. (2 respondents or 3% have obtained legal divorce).

Inspite of their awareness of legal divorce, the majority have not sought legal divorce. The reasons for not seeking legal divorce indicate that, among the working majority of the respondents (28%) have not sought it due to the various attitudes and pressures the society imposes on a divorced woman. 22% of the respondents said they were not interested in subjecting themselves to the lenthly legal procedures involving heavy expenditure, both of which they could ill-afford. The rest, 20% of the respondents, either want to reconcile with their husbands or they do not want to obtain the divorce, for the sake of children, or they wish to save themselves from the pressures of a legal divorce. (30% of the working respondents have currently applied).

The reasons given by most of the non-working respondents are in the order of apathy towards obtaining divorce (28%), inability to go to the courts (26%) husbands not being co-operative and hence unable to apply for a divorce (8%).

30% of the respondents however desire reconciliation with

their husbands and therefore do not want to apply for a divorce.

The remaining 8% of the respondents have not applied for a legal divorce as they either do not know the whereabouts of the husbands or they have sought the help of women's organisations to get a divorce.

In conclusion more non-working respondents want to reconcile with their husbands than working respondents. The findings of Ram Mehta are relevant to the findings of this study :

"Though most of the respondents have a knowledge of legislation, the knowledge was such that they could not assess its benefits. A sense of shame and failure to admit that marriage has broken coupled with high cost in getting the divorce, and money involved in seeking divorce prevents most of them from seeking it."

Hazards faced in obtaining a divorce

Measures suggested to simplify Legal Procedure. Though very few respondents in the sample were legally divorced, in order to assess the problems they endure they were asked to detail their problems and the measures they would suggest to simplify the legal procedures.

Working respondents said that they not only had to spend a huge amount of money, they were subjected to immense physical and mental strain.

Often the advocates who dealt with their case, took advantage of them and exorted huge amounts of money at regular intervals on the pretext of fighting their case.

Some respondents even confessed that long years of waiting, frequent visits to the court, and the consequent exposure often made them feel regretful for having ventured going to the court.

Only two respondents did not face much trouble in getting a legal divorce as they had sufficient evidence against their husbands. While in the case of one respondent it was a divorce by mutual consent, in the other case it was religious separation.

Among the non-working group the two respondents who obtained legal divorce did not face any problems as the divorce was sanctioned on mutual consent.

Both the groups suggested certain measures for simplifying the legal procedure for obtaining divorce easily.

One of the measures suggested was the setting up of separate courts to deal exclusively with divorce cases. The other suggestion was the need to implement the family courts act, for the quick disposal of cases. Surprisingly there was a working respondent who could not make any suggestion to give relief to women seeking legal divorce.

Conclusion. From the above discussed points, it is clearly eident that women face immense problems in obtaining a legal divorce. As such, it is high time the government took note of the above points, and legislated certain measures for the easy disposal of the cases.

(iii) Case Studies of Working and Non-Working Divorced/ Separated Women

Introduction. A few selected case studies from both working and non-working categories are given below. These case studies highlight the traumatic experience they undergo in the course of a separation or divorce, the status they hold at their homes, at the work place and in society and the unique problems they face as single women.

Working Divorced/Separated Women—Case Study No. 1

Dark, tall and extremely talkative, Seema Williams is a 42 year old divorced women. She belongs to an upper middle class family of two brothers and two sisters of whom she is the youngest.

They are Malayalam speaking protestant Christians belonging originally to Kerala state, but having now settled in Bangalore city. Her father was a military officer and mother a teacher. Her two brothers are well qualified and hold high positions in the government.

Both Seema and her elder sister are post graduate degree holders. While her sister recently retired from service as a teacher in a school, Seema continues to be in service as a teacher in a corporation high school. She earns an income of Rs. 1500 per month.

Seema's experience is indeed pathetic. Her trauma began during her childhood itself. She recalls being a neglected child. Her mother always ill-treated her, deprived her of the love and affection which she longed for. Seema feels that her mother was distinctly partial to her sister showering her with much love and affection. This created a rift between the two sisters as a consequence of which apart from rivalry there was jealously and bitterness between them. She developed the negative feelings of anger and hatred particularly, towards her mother, and wanting to show her mother and sister that she could live on her own, she looked for love and affection outside the home.

It was was during this phase that Seema developed a close friendship with her collegemate, who paid her a lot of attention and gave her the warmth that she sought. She also gave her gifts. Little did Seema know that her friend was deceiving her with an ulterior motive in mind.

Knowing Seema's sad, lonely childhood and feigning sympathy towards her, her friend proposed that Seema marry her brother, who was highly qualified and well employed. Seema did not know that in fact her friend's brother was of ill-repute and highly irresponsible. She agreed to marry her brother, partly because she wanted to spite her mother and sister and partly to show that she was capable of leading her own life without any assistance from them.

Blissfully unaware of the problems that she would encounter, Seema stepped into her matrimonial home weaving dreams of a happy home built on love and affection. But to her dismay she found her husband not only uneducated but also unemployed. The entire responsibility of managing the household and maintaining her husband fell on her.

Though inwardly shocked, Seema put up a brave front to the outside world and faced all odds that came her way with courage. She made efforts to educate her husband and secure him gainful employment through friends and well wishers.

However, being extremely irresponsible her husband was not interested either in gaining education or securing a job. He constantly demanded money from his working wife and if she failed to comply with his demands he humiliated and tortured her physically.

Seema suffered all the hurt, humiliation and insults, hoping that realisation would dawn upon him and he would change for the better. She put up with him for 16 years. Seema confesses that during this period her husband deserted her several times, each time she tried to patch up the differences between them as she did not want others to know about their disharmonious marital life. She also confessed that her husband was a sexual pervert for which she detested him deeply.

The only streak of brightness in her dark life was the birth of her daughter. For the first time in her life she could experience some happiness. Seeing the little baby she could forget all her heart-ache, agony and mental anguish. She continued to cohabit with her husband, for the sake of the child and the society. She did not reveal even to her parents the hardships she had undergone because of her husband.

But, when her husband, inspite of her attempts to correct him, continued to harass and to torture her physically, even in the presence of her daughter, she decided to divorce him. She consulted several lawyers and filed a case for divorce on the grounds of physical and mental cruelty.

Her husband ran away from home and married a Muslim woman. The legal procedure took 3 years before she could obtain a decree or divorce from the court.

Seema is currently staying with her daughter and son-in-law who were married recently. Though legally free from her husband Seema is not free from being exploited. Her own daughter and son-in-law extract both money and work from her. Compelled to spend all her savings on them and further drain herself in physical work, Seema seems to have little faith in 'human beings'. At the work place also she considers herself the focus of discussion among her colleagues. She reported that several men teachers in the school tried to molest her sexually. According to Seema "to be born a woman is a curse and to be single is a double curse". She further relates that single women are not allowed to be happy. They are not even permitted to dress and move about with respect.

Racapitulating, Seema says that life has never been kind to her. Ill-treated by mother, tortured by husband, mocked at by colleagues and exploited by her daughter, she never had peace in life.

An enquiry into her future plans reveals that at present she is friendly with a Brahmin boy. Though he has been pressing her to marry him she discounts the possibility of marriage. With the bitter experience of one marriage haunting her, Seema fears to plunge into another

The above case history of the respondent reveals that she has displayed laudable courage in facing the problems she encountred in life. She has refused to accept her situation as destiny by battling along without any moral support. Very few single women display the kind of strength which Seema has displayed.

Working Divorced/Separated Women—Case Study No. 2

35 year old Gayatri is a soft spoken, mild-natured women. She comes from an upper middle class family of five sisters who are all well educated and placed in life. All her sisters are married and living with their spouses. Gayatri also being highly educated holds a post-graduate degree and is employed as a secretary in a private company with a salary of Rs 1200 per month.

Like her sisters, Gayatri's marriage was arranged with a person belonging to their own caste. She was 24 years of age at the time. He was highly qualified with a degree in business management and employed abroad. Unaware of the fate that was in store for them Gayatri's parents were overjoyed at the prospect of having got a good match for their daughter.

Gayatri's marriage was celebrated with grandeur. Her father gave her jewellery, household articles, furniture and cash as dowry. Unfortunately for Gayatri even after meeting all the wedding demands marriage turned out to be a rattling experience. To her surprise she found her husband to be a habitual gambler and a very irresponsible person who gambled away all the money and articles given to her during her marriage.

He stayed in India for 4 years after marriage during which period he gambled away everything that he could lay his hands on to the extent that there was not a thing of value left in the house. Apart from this he also took loans from various sources and without repaying them he left the country promising her and the children that he would be back soon. However Gayatri has not heard from him for the last four years. She is unable to trace him, though she has made several attempts to locate his whereabouts through friends abroad.

Disillusioned by her husband, steeped in debts, harassed by money-lenders and unable to maintain the family, she took up a job in a company in the private sector.

At present she is living with her daughters in a house gifted to her by her father. Though financially she is self-supporting, Gayatri, due to the dramatic experiences she has undergone, has been left with permanent emotional scars. It has made her cynical to the extent that she distrusts the whole human race. Added to her many problems Gayatri says that society also does not allow her to live in peace. Though separated for more than four years she is one of those unfortunate women who is exploited financially by in-laws instead of being helped by them. Gayatri avers that despite her efforts to curtail any contact with her parents in-law and brother-in-law, they constantly visit her house. Their visits are gain based. They expect her to treat them cordially and spend extravagently on them, and give them money on demand. She also complained that her brother-in-law tries to take advantage of her living alone with her young children. He once tried to assault her sexually but she was miraculously saved by the timely visit of her friends She is unable to prevent him coming home without exposing him. Thus she is in constant fear.

At the work place her colleagues are unaware about details of her personal life. However, she has informed them that her husband is abroad. This has helped her to have a fairly peaceful atmosphere in the work place. Tensed and disturbed, her main worry is about the future of her children. She fears that being single she may not be able to give them the 'best' in life.

Asked about her own plans for the future Gayatri says she has none for herself. She wants her children to grow up into healthy human beings unaffected by the failure of her own marriage.

Non-Working Divorced/Separated Women—Case Study

Sunita is a 30 year old Hindu Brahmin who separated from her husband about two years ago. Her family consists of her mother and younger sister. Her mother is also separated from her husband ; he is a mentally unsound person, living away from the family.

Sunita was educated by her uncle who helped her to do her graduation and was employed in a factory even before her marriage.

Sunita's marriage was arranged by her uncle to a man belonging to her caste. Being technically qualified and employed in a Government establishment his income exceeded Rs. 3000 per month. As such the condition put by the groom was that Sunita resign her job before the marriage and accordingly Sunita left the job.

To perform the marriage the family spent Rs. 50,000 in cash apart from gold ornaments, silver and other household articles for her.

For two years after marriage Sunita lived in her husband's house along with his mother. Unfortunately her mother-in-law was a great source of trouble to their marital happiness. This, according to Sunita, might have been due to her own failure in marriage. She also learnt that her mother-in-law was an irresponsible woman who had run away from her husband when she was expecting her only child, i.e, her husband. Therefore she was greatly attached to her only son. She could not tolerate any other person in her son's life. The respondent's husband was also equally attached to his mother and had never disobeyed or caused any unhappiness to her.

The immense attachment of mother and son was responsible for a rift in the husband-and-wife relationship. Sunita's mother-in-law never gave them an opportunity to talk or go out together. She monopolised all her son's time, right from talking to going out for an evening walk. Thus gradually there was little communication between them and Sunita felt totally isolated. This apart, her mother-in-law went to the extent of complaining against her as a result of which her husband became indifferent and cold towards her. Sunita sees her mother-in-law as a selfish, mean and possessive woman. And at times she felt that she was abnormal, at times she even feared being alone with her. Not satisfied with what was offered at the time of marriage Sunita avers that her mother-in-law also forced her to bring more dowry.

The mother and son often jointly ill-treated Sunita. Their indifferent and inconsiderate attitude, especially that of her husband, greatly hurt her.

Her mother-in-law's possessive nature crossed all limits when she kept her son physically away from Sunita. Her husband being timid by nature did not object to even this separation. Thus the respondent being unable to bear the humiliation meted out to her sought refuge at her parents' house.

Consequently she is living with her mother. Some of her friends tried to bring reconciliation between her and her husband. But the adamant, negative attitude of the mother-in-law and her sustained domination over her son did not help in bringing them together.

Sunita has informed her husband that she is willing to give her marriage a second chance if he is agreeable and willing to set up a separate house. However she, feels her husband is too meek to take such a bold step.

Though looked after well by her parents, Sunita considers herself a burden to her mother. She is sorry that she resigned her job and is now looking for a suitable job so that she can live independently with her daughter. She also feels that the chances of her younger sister's marriage have been considerably reduced because of her separation and her residing in her mother's house.

Sunita says, "As a separated woman I have to face a lot of humiliation from my relatives". Therefore she minimises her social life, and so feels lonely and deserted. Being unemployed and socially at a disadvantage she constantly worries about the future.

An enquiry into the possibility of a remarriage reveals that Sunita holds no such plans but she does not rule out the possibility of a reconciliation with her husband if he agreed to her condition of setting up an independent house. Sunita hopes that sometime her husband will be able to break away from his ever-dominant mother and live with her. For the fulfilment of this fond hope and her daughter she lives.

Non-Working Divorced/Separated Women—Case Study No. 2.

Ragini, a 37 year old Balija Christian girl, comes from a lower middle class family. Though she hails from a small sized family of four members only, she has received very little education. This is basically due to her disinterest in acquiring education. Her mother now a widow, is totally dependent on the respondent's only brother who has an independent business.

Ragini was hardly 18 years old when she fell in love with a Bengali Christian boy living in the same locality. Her mother did not oppose Ragini's wish to marry this boy as he was employed in a public sector company as a security guard earning Rs. 600 per month. Further her mother was incapable of looking for a suitable groom and meeting dowry demands.

But there was much resentment towards this alliance by members of the boy's family. His parents wanted him to marry a girl from a well-to-do family who could meet their dowry demands. However, the boy being adamant in his decision, they were married. For this, his parents were very unhappy and probably, according to Ragini, made up their mind to break their marriage. They constantly tried to brainwash their son against his wife.

Her husband being the sole earning member of the family comprising several younger brothers and sisters, finance was always a constraint.

Being continuously faced with financial problems coupled with complaints regarding his wife, the respondent's husband vent his frustrations on the respondent. She was humiliated and nagged for not making any attempt to seek a job and contribute to the family income.

Unable to get a job due to her inadequate education and skills, but eager to work out her marriage, Ragini wanting some happiness, in her married life requested her brother to get a loan in order to help her husband overcome his financial crisis.

Ragini's brother managed to raise Rs. 10,000 from various sources which she gave to her husband. What she did not know or even suspect was that her husband had developed an affair with another woman. On receiving the amount, he deserted her and set up a home with the other woman. He had even taken away all her personal belongings to give them as a gift to her.

The respondent was immensely shocked at his behaviour towards her. Her in-laws had succeeded in poisoning their son's mind against her and in consequence broke their marriage. They started ill-treating and torturing her to further drive her away from their house. Unable to bear the physical and mental agony she was subjected to, the respondent finally went to live in her mother's house.

Steeped in debts and with no means of subsistence the respondent feels totally dejected. She with the assistance of her brother has consulted a lawyer and has filed a criminal case against her husband. She vows that she will never reconcile with her husband.

Asked about her future plans, Ragini says that she, with some apprenticeship training under the guidance of her brother, has now become a partner in his business and intends to set up her own independent venture after a few years.

Being alone, also childless, Ragini's history indicates how her husbands's unkind, inconsiderate and irresponsible attitude and behaviour has destroyed the life of girl at a very young age.

6

The Status of Single Women

Introduction. The position and status of women in Indian society is not encouraging. The birth of a female child itself is an occasion of sorrow and not of joy. A girl is brought up in a sheltered and protected manner with the sole idea of getting her married at the earliest. Marriage seems the end for which a girl has to be groomed. As such, a married woman is considered virtuous and respectable and therefore accorded a high place in society. Having been brought up in such an atmosphere attempts to deviate from the normal conventions of the society are usually scorned. Under such circumstances the plight and suffering of women who remain single due to various reasons is indeed deplorable.

The causes for remaining single could be either voluntary or circumstantial. Women who chose to remain single voluntarily include those who have remained unmarried out of their own free will and among the married women, those who have separated or divorced from their husband due to various reasons.

Women who are single due to circumstantial factors include those who are unmarried because of family circumstances such as the inability to raise dowry, illness, lack of good looks, etc. Married women who have become single due to circumstances are the widowed and those who have been deserted by their husbands against their will.

Whether the decision to remain single is voluntary or involuntary these women are generally looked down upon inspite of their living with their parents, parents-in law siblings or children. The absence of marriage among the unmarried and that of a husband or household head among the married makes them extremely vulnerable to problems—social, psychological, economic and sexual. Being single is therefore a taboo. They are neglected, humiliated, harassed and accordingly doled out the least status in the society. They are condemned for defying the conventions of the society.

Even unmarried women who might have chosen a career instead of a home life, independence and freedom to chains of bondage in marriage are rebuked and considered as social deviants. Their professional success is often seen with suspicion and their moral behaviour is the focus of almost all discussion.

In the case of widows, it is not self-imposed singleness, having lost their husbands they are regarded as inauspicious and sinful women. Considered a burden, especially if with dependent children, they are at the mercy of those who grudgingly agree to take care of them. A lot of restrictions are imposed on them with absolutely little or no freedom to either speak or act as they want. They are treated by society as an insufferable appendage.

The divorced or separated women (whether imposed or voluntary) are also regarded with suspicion. Women who fail to live through a marriage partnership though it is an unhappy or even a brutal relationship are rejected by society. Even where the break in marriage is initiated by the husband it is always the women's behaviour that is questioned and the man receives the sympathy and suport of the society.

Whatever the category of singleness, i.e, unmarried, widows divorced/separated whether self imposed or circumstantial, young or old, working or non-working the problems they face are almost similar, with variation only in intensity and not in kind.

Socially they are boycotted and victimised, psychologically they are subjected to innumerable mental tensions, sexually they are totally vulnerable and added to this if they are economically dependent they find themselves doubly abused and exploited.

In view of the taboo and stigma attached to singlehood and the negative attitude of the society towards a significant section of its women and their consequent alienation there arises a need to understand the problems that these women face from their own view point. Having made an indepth study of them a comparative analysis of isolate groups is made in order to highlight the extent and intensity of the problems they face and to identify the areas of maximum exploitation of these sections of women. This could be followed by suggestions to the government and non-governmental agencies interested in their welfare and whose intentions are in the direction of assimilating them into the main stream of society.

(i) Comparative analysis of single w omen

The age profile of the respondents indicates that whether working or non-working women who are spinsters belong to the relatively younger age groups of 35 to 40 yrs (66% and 61%) The operational definition adopted for spinsters for this study is 35 years and above.

Among the working widows, 90% of them are below the age of 50 years whereas among the non-working 84% are above the age of 50 years. Working widows are younger than non-working widows. Probably, their young age at the time of widowhood had made it possible for them to enter the labour market.

As regards divorced/separated it is observed that among both the working or non-working categories the majority of the respondents are below 40 years (74% and 88% respectively). Again a higher proportion of working divorced/separated are younger than of non-working. Being relatively young in age, and economically independent most of the working women seem to have divorced or separated. The incidence of divorce and separation is high among the young and economically independent women.

The general observation therefore is that working single women belong to a relatively younger age group than non-working single women. Divorce being a new phenomenon, its incidence is again higher among the young and working categories.

The pattern of migration among single women reveals that the majority of them are non migrant. This characteristic is to

TABLE A.1

Age Distribution among Single Women

Age Group	*Spinsters*		*Widows*		*Divorced/Separated*	
	Working	*Non-working*	*Working*	*Non-working*	*Working*	*Non-working*
Below 25 yrs	—	—	2	—	10	34
26 yrs to 30 yrs	—	—	1	3	21	24
31 yrs to 35 yrs	—	—	19	3	27	19
36 yrs to 40 yrs	66	61	23	5	16	12
41 yrs to 45 yrs	19	31	19	5	18	3
46 yrs to 50 yrs	13	—	19	6	3	3
51 yrs to 55 yrs	—	4	8	18	5	6
56 yrs to 60 yrs	2	—	2	13	—	—
61 yrs and above	—	4	—	47	—	—
Total	100	100	100	100	100	100

TABLE A.2

Migration Pattern among Single Women

Migration	*Spinsters*		*Widows*		*Divorced/Separated*	
	Working	*Non-working*	*Working*	*Non-working*	*Working*	*Non-working*
1. Not Migrated	52	83	58	66	68	61
2. Migration within the State	29	13	29	29	19	34
3. Migration outside the State	12	4	13	5	13	5
4. Outside the country Others	7	—	—	—	—	—
	100%	100	100	100	100	100

a greater extent observed among non-working spinsters and widows (88% and 66%). However, among the divorced/separated a higher proportion of working than non-working respondents are non-migrants.

Where migration exists it is inter-state migration that is the most common pattern. In case of inter-state migration it is most noticeable among the working women. Thus it is observed that migration from other regions or states is generally low among the single women especially among those who are non-working.

In consonance with the religion-wise profile of the country the analysis of the data shows that Hindus form the predominant group among all the three categories of both working and non-working followed by that of Christians and Muslims.

A comparative analysis of the educational attainments of single women indicates that in general working single women have higher educational qualifications than non-working single women. Among spinsters a higher proportion of working women (59%) have received college education than of non-working (26%).

So also among working divorced/separated women 50% of them have received college education as against 23% among non-working. However, among the working widows the majority of them (41%) have had high school education, sufficient enough to enter the labour market. Non-working widows have received less than high school education. Most of them are educated only up to upper primary level (63%) thus making it difficult for them to enter the labour force. In general single women who are employed are better educated than the non-working.

The observed minimum level of education found to be necessary to seek gainful employment in a country like India is at least Matriculation. Taking this level as the base line ratios have been drawn to compare the educational background of working and non-working single women. It is interesting to note that for every one educated non-working single woman there are one, two and three working spinsters, divorced/separated add widowed women respectively. This clearly indicates that the search for employment among spinsters and divorced/separated is that of choice. The trend among widows however is that of compulsion on economics grounds.

Education being co-related to employment in general it has been noticed that working women who have higher education are employed in better jobs and are earning higher incomes. Spinsters and divorced/separated women having acquired higher education consequently are employed in higher paying occupations. They are basically employed as clerks, teachers and executives. In contrast, the widows having basically received less education seem to be employed as operators, ayahs and peons.

In view of their better qualifications, working spinsters and divorced/separated women are able to generate more income. Their income ranges between Rs. 1000 to Rs. 2500 per month as against that of working widows whose income range is between Rs. 300 to 500 per month.

Working widows seem to have sought employment only after their husband's death. Endowed with less or no education they have not been able to secure high income-generating jobs. They have sought and got employment mostly on compassionate grounds. In view of their joining the labour market due to dire economic need most of them are able to earn very low incomes as compared to working spinsters and working divorced/separated women. Entry into the labour market is marked by their own choice and decision to be employed.

The higher education level and consequently higher income of working spinsters has largely influenced their decision to remain single and in the case of the working divorced and separated women, their decisions to either separate or divorce from their husbands.

The educational attainment of individuals generally being the function of home environment, here expressed in terms of the educational attainment of other members in the family, an attempt has been made to evaluate their general educational standard. The education of youngsters in the family is to a great extent influenced by the parents.

An educational index for the family was developed giving weightage to each level of education, and cut off points were then drawn in order to categorise the households as either less, moderately or highly educated households. Households with a total weightage of 1 to 4 were categorised as less educated households. The members of such households were found to

TABLE A.3

Educational Qualification of Single Women

Educational Qualification	*Spinsters*		*Widows*		*Divorced/Separated*	
	Working	*Non-working*	*Working*	*Non-working*	*Working*	*Non-working*
Illiterate	—	—	6	14	5	2
Primary Education	4	17	34	63	16	27
High School/Inter P.U.C.	37	57	41	18	29	48
College Education	59	26	19	5	50	23
	100	100	100	100	100	100

have less than high school education. Households whose score ranged between 5 and 7 points were grouped under moderately educated households. The majority of the members of such households possessed education ranging between matriculation or intermediate. Finally households scoring a weightage of 8 and above were classed as highly educated households. Members in these households have graduate education and above.

The position of the members of the parental families on the educational index among these groups indicates a definite co-relation between the personal educational attainment of the respondents themselves and their families. The observation is that the members of the working spinsters' and divorced/separated women's groups have a higher educational index than working widows. As such a higher proportion of the families of working widows (45%) belong to medium or low educated group households. Again it is noticed that the educational index of the family members of working single women is higher than non-working single women.

This indicates that the members of the families of working as against non-working and spinsters and divorced/separated women as against widows possess relatively more education.

Marriage in India being mostly an union of two families rather than of two individuals it is common that alliances are generally sought for daughters into families of either equal or higher standing. This ensures for the daughters similar class conditions or mobility into higher groups.

Occupation and income being functions of education, further an attempt was made to study the educational index of the husband's families and members of the households of the husband's families. The analysis refers only to respondents who are either widows or divorced/separated women.

Divorced/separated women who belong to the highly educated category in the educational index of the parental families have gone into families of similar index (i.e. highly educated group households). Correspondingly working widows with low or medium educational index from the parental families have similarly married into low or medium education group households.

The educational index of the families in which the respondents are currently residing was also taken into consideration. While there is a consistency in the educational level between the parental families and that of their husbands' there is a definite shift is the educational index of their current families. In the current families a majority of both working and non-working spinsters belong to the high education group households.

In the case of working widows and both working and non-working divorced/separated women the highest proportion of households belongs to the low education group. Their percentage being 48 and 58 and 47 respectively. On the other hand a majority of the members of the non-working widows belong to the high education index group i.e. 63%.

This pattern is due to the influence of several factors like (1) size of the family, (2) number of children and (3) the age of the children.

Non-working widows belonging mainly to the older age groups have older children who have acquired higher education and hold a higher position on the educational index. On the other hand most of the working widows, divorced/separated have dropped on the educational index mainly because of the fact that the majority of the respondents have either no children or have very young children who are studying in schools.

A large number of divorced/separated women are staying independently in hostels. In such households the educational index of only the respondent is taken into account. As such the index is only medium.

Further financial gains being a direct outcome of the educational attainment of an individual an attempt has been made to study the financial status of the respondents in terms of the position vis-a-vis the poverty line. Information collected from the seventh five year plan 1985-90 from the planning Department of Government of Karnataka for urban industrial workers for the year 1983, fixes the average consumption amount at Rs. 523 per month. This has been taken as the demarcating line to group the families by income and categorise them as those below and above the poverty line.

The majority of both working spinsters' and divorced/separated parental families are above the poverty line (52% and 42% respectively) and a higher proportion of working and non-working widows' families (77% and 42%) and non-working divorced/separated families are below the poverty line.

The per capita income of both parental and current families of working spinsters is higher than non-working spinsters. There is more upward mobility from below to above the poverty line from the parental to the current family situation among working spinsters than among non-working spinster households. This is because a majority of the parental families belong to the medium size households whereas in the current families a large number of families belong to the small size household category. Per capita income being directly dependent on the size of the family the higher per capita income in working spinsters' households is largely due to high status of the family members on the educational index and thereby higher incomes. Inspite of the small size of the families of non-working spinsters the per capita income is low due to the combined effect of less education and employment of members in low paid jobs.

The majority of the parents' families of working widows are below the poverty line (77%). In the non-working widows' households 42% are below the poverty line. This does not indicate higher per capita income in these families as information on this aspect is not available for nearly 40% of the households.

In view of the low education and occupation and low income generating jobs a higher percentage of the working widows are below the poverty line than non-working widows. (77%)

The current financial status of working widows indicates that 77% are below the poverty line as compared to 68% of non-working widows. Per capita income being a co-relate to the size of the family an analysis of the size of the family shows that the majority of working widows (56%) belong to small size families, i.e., 1 to 4 members. Among non-working widows the majority (52%) belong to small size families i.e. to 1 to 4 member while (43%) belong to medium sized families.

Thus current families of non-working widows, though medium sized, enjoy a higher standard of living mainly because they have grown up children with higher levels of education and high income-generating employment whereas the working widows who have very young children are unable to maintain high standards of living.

Regarding the parental families of divorced/separated women it is seen that 48% of working respondents are below the poverty line as against 72% of the parents' families of the non-working respondents. The very high proportion of non-working respondents in their parental families living in extremely poor conditions may be due to a considerable percentage of them coming from large sized households.

In the current family situation 40% and 66% of the households of working and non-working respondents respectively are below the poverty line.

Here again an analysis of the size of the families indicates that 69% of the respondents of the non-working households are small sized and the decrease in the proportion of respondents below poverty line from parental to current families may be due to the shift in the size of the families from large to small sized households.

The financial status of the family was further judged by the value of assets that they possessed. An index was developed to estimate the worth of the assets and weightages were given to assets and accordingly households were grouped into nil or low asset group, medium asset group, and high asset group households.

Between working and non-working, a higher proportion of working spinsters belong to the medium and high asset group than non-working spinsters, indicating a relatively better financial position among working spinsters.

Among working widows there is no significant difference in the possession of assets between parental, husband and current households. They belong to the low asset group in all the three categories of households In the case of non-working widows there is a shift from the low asset group in their parental households to medium or high asset group in their husband's and current households. They are economically well off because they have older children who are well employed and whose income has been useful in accumulating assets.

As regards the divorced or separated women the highest percentage of households among the working respondents belong to the middle asset group in their parental households, nil asset group in their husbands' households and low asset group in their current position. Among the non-working respondents the majority of both the parents' and husbands' families belong to the low asset groups while in their current position they belong to the nil asset group. The sudden shift in their marital status from that of a married woman to either a separated or divorced woman might have been responsible for their low or nil possession of assets.

In general, parental families of working respondents seem to be financially better off than that of the families of their husbands. But in comparison to that of husbands' families their current families seem to be slightly improved.

To conclude, working spinsters have a higher financial status in view of their better education and income generating occupations The financial condition of the non-working spinsters, however, is very much lower because of their relatively low education and lack of earning power.

Working widows on the other hand face immense financial problems because of their low education, late entry into the labour market and low income. Besides they have young children to be supported. The financial position of working widows seems to be worse compared to the non-working This does not mean that non-working widows suffer less. Considering their age and the presence of employed children, a reflection indicates that they must have suffered even more than the current young working widows. This being mainly due to their having to support their children in the absence of an independent income.

The financial condition of working divorced/separated respondents is slightly better than that of those non-working. Working respondents having received higher education and earning a larger income (unlike the non-working with less education and remaining unemployed). are able to maintain a higher standard of living. Divorce/separation is therefore more of an imposed burden on those unemployed.

(ii) Findings of the Study

The following paragraphs discuss the problems these three categories of single women face in the various social environments i.e., family, workspot and society.

TABLE A.4

Poverty Line in the Current Families of Single Women

P.L.	*Spinsters*		*Widows*		*Divorced/Separated*	
	Working	*Non-Working*	*Working*	*Non-Working*	*Working*	*Non-Working*
Below Poverty line Below Rs. 532 p.m.	35	61	77	68	50	66
Above Poverty line Above Rs. 533 p.m.	65	26	23	32	42	11
N.A.D K.	—	13	—	—	8	23
Total	100	100	100	100	108	100

These problems, however, differ in intensity depending on several variables like age, religion or caste, education, employment, income and their socio-economic background. Though certain problems are common to all single women, the study reveals that the young, and those with nil or little education, and those unemployed face greater problems than those who are older in age and those educated, employed and to a certain extent economically independent.

To get an overall perspective of the problems faced by single women, they are classified under major headings. They are :

1. Psychological problems,
2. Economic problems,
3. Problems at home and work,
4. Social problems.

The degree or the intensity of the problem differs for different categories of single women.

The percentage-wise distribution of respondents by problems faced among both working and non-working single women has been presented in Table A.5. In a society where many of the problems are viewed in the context of financial constraints it is interesting to note that to working respondents and even to those non-working the major area of problems are of a psychological nature. A majority of the single women though facing other socio-economic problems have in one voice emphasized the psychological trauma which they undergo as a result of being single.

This problem manifests itself in either loneliness, insecurity and consequent depression or desertion. Such negative emotions and continuous suppression of feelings effects the over all physical and mental well-being of the individuals which makes them withdraw themselves from society. But it is the attitude and reaction of the society which has been responsible for their unique behaviour. If society continues to reject them it will be reinforcing their lonelines and its allied insecurities, thus affecting their potential to contribute to the development of society. Under such circumstances it is important that society treats single women with dignity, love, understanding and as fellow human beings.

The second major area of problem is that of finance. The status and position an individual holds in society is largely determined by her economic status. The data reveals that economically independent single women face economic problems to a lesser degree than those totally economically dependent. And among the single women, spinsters with no responsibilities have less economic problems than those widowed and divorced or or separated who have to support and maintain very young children. It is observed also that among working spinsters almost 85% of them face no problems. Non-working Widows at present face less financial problems because of the presence of older children who bring in an income. Thus due to the immense economic insecurity most of them feel deprived of status in both their own family circles and society in general.

At the time of duress, the initial and spontaneous support single women seek is that of their parents. Unfortuately even in their parental homes most women face problems. If they are unmarried they are treated as a life long burden and therefore a liability. The constant reference to their single state creates tensions among the family members often leading to quarrels and lack of peace. Such a treatment creates a sense of desertion in the minds of single women causing severe psychological problems. Due to the unhealthy atmosphere in the home they are subjected to immense agony resulting in their isolating themselves from other family members.

If employed they are expected to hand over their entire income to their parents without any expectation in return or even appreciation for this financial support. If unemployed their condition is worse. Where the employed spinster's needs are met grudgingly, those of the unemployed are met to the minimum basic extent.

The widowed women though treated with sympathy by the members of their family often are not accorded a high status even within the family. Certain restrictions are imposed on them in terms of dress or wearing decorative ornaments or participating in social ceremonies. She is considered as a woman who has sinned ; and is regarded with suspicion and as an ill omen, and therefore encouraged to participate in religious activities. Thus on the grounds of widowhood they are deprived of all their extra needs and their movements are restricted.

Whether economically dependent or independent they are expected to work the whole day in the kitchen for the sake of the other family members. They are taken for granted and no effort is made by any one in the family to help them to carry out the household duties. Even if employed they are expected to contribute to the family income, and to household duties.

However, if they are older in age and are employed they are consulted on several issues concerning their children.

The divorced/separated women face greater problems than either widows or spinsters. This is specially true in cases where women take the initiative for divorce or separation. She is denied both sympathy and support for having failed to make necessary adjustments and is often blamed for the breakdown of marriage Shouldering such blame divorced/separated avoid attending or participating in social ceremonies due to the fear of social gossip or boycott. Their parents fear to support them as they are apprehensive of getting suitable grooms for other unmarried daughters in the family because of the unaccepted behaviour of those who have undergone separation or divorce.

If unemployed and with children they are regarded as a burden and if working, though their position is slightly better, they are expected to manage their households all by themselves, often ridiculed they are more scorned than respected.

In general, a comparative analysis of the status in society of these single women reveals that unmarried women have a slightly better position, followed by divorced or separated women and widows. This is because women (Kanya Muthaithua) though unmarried, in certain communities in India are regarded as "maiden Sumangalis" and therefore auspicious and accorded a status in society, and secondly, divorced or separated, though separated from husbands are also regarded as Sumangalis and they therefore enjoy certain privileges that a married women in society is entitled to. The status of widows is far inferior to either of these single women because they are considered as unfortunate women, whose sins have brought them widowhood.

The system of exploitation does not end in the family but

is extended outside, i.e., at the work place and society. Working women are exposed to the outside world. Being single they become vulnerable, they are victimised and viewed by men as an object of pleasure. If separated or divorced they are considered as highly deviant women who are on the lookout for new ventures. On the one hand they are looked on with suspicion and on the other hand as morally loose women. While widows are sympathized with for their misfortune no chance is left unexplored to exploit them. Sometimes they are lured and often victimized.

Exploited by men at the work place and deprived of a respectable position in society they are not spared by their fellow women colleagues who subject them to unhealthy discussion on their personal lives so that it upsets their mental balance.

Thus it is seen that none of the problems exist in isolation. They are interlinked and one perpetuates the other. Under the circumstances it is important to understand and suggest measures to help them minimise their problems and lead a happy life in society. In this connection it was felt that no outsider can have an insight into the intensity of their problems as they themselves can. As such it becomes obvious that relief meaures are best explained by them as per their needs. The following are the suggestions made by the singles for their welfare.

From all the 3 categories most of them have unanimously suggested the need for setting up homes for single women. The next important suggestion is the need to render financial help in order to reduce their sufferings. There should be a conscious mobilisation of awareness among all sections of the society starting from the family as a unit to overcome certain misconceptions and practices connected with single women in society and treat them with human dignity and understanding.

(iii) Recommendations

In the light of the above discussions certain socio-legislative measures have been suggested to alleviate the sufferings of single women.

Though the Constitution of India guarantees equal rights and opportunities to women in India, in reality the life of women is steeped in misery and subjugation. This is specially true of single women who are further exploited and victimised.

The Indian woman of today should fight against the existing prejudices against women and should force herself from the secondary status that is accorded to her in this male-dominated society. This struggle being one of a continuous nature, it should begin in the homes where the socialisation of both male and female starts. It becomes very essential that the right social values should be inculcated from childhood which should begin at birth itself. At the outset social prejudices against the birth of a female child and indiscriminate killing of female children are against the dignity and status of women. Parents should provide equal opportunities to both female and male children, and in no time during the life of a girl should she be regarded as a liability and inferior to a boy.

The ideas that careers are for boys and marriage for girls should be wiped out. Marriage should not be made as the ultimate aim of a girl's life. Daughters who want to remain unmarried for various reasons, like to pursue a career, should be encouraged and their unmarried status should in no way cause an impediment to progress in their career or in their personal life

If for other reasons beyond their own control, like family circumstances or dowry problem, they choose to remain single they should not only be treated with respect and dignity but also be appreciated for the sacrifices they willingly make for the sake of other members in the family, thus helping them to lead a respectable life.

As regards the widows, the taboos and restrictions imposed on widows are indeed pathetic. Condemned by society they are forced to lead a miserable life until their death, unlike a widower who remarries even before the funeral pyre of his wife cools down.

Widow remarriage should be encouraged to enable young childless widows and also those with children to remarry to give them financial and emotional support in their life.

Education and technological innovation have brought about a great deal of changes in society. But it is unfortunate that the concept of widow remarriage is yet to gain popular support and the approval of society.

The attitude of society towards widow remarriage needs to be changed. The concept advocated by social reformers from the 19th century should be widely accepted by the society.

The concept of divorce or separation being relatively a novel phenomena in Indian society, in general there is a greater need for understanding of the problems faced by these women.

Singlehood is looked down upon in Indian socity. Marriage being the ultimate goal of their lives women are taught to tolerate and overcome the stress and strains of marital relationships even under the worst conditions.

This is because women once married are considered as a property lost. A woman who breaks marriage does not receive the sympathy or support of the parents or her siblings. On the other hand she has to constantly face the rage of society. Thus due to the fear of being subjected to intense psycho-socio problems most women, though they face several conflicts, prefer to live in a marriage than out of it. Thus it is only under severe conditions that the breakdown of marriage takes place. Under such circumstances greater sympathy should be given to women.

In fact it is better for a woman to live separately than to live with an incompatible partner in a non-existing relationship.

Women who want to break away from unhappy marriages ought to be given a dissolution to enable them to re-marry or to lead the life of their own choice. The lengthy legal procedures which affect the mental-physical well-being of divorced and separated women need to be made simple and efficient.

In general separated or divorced women who choose a life of diginity and self respect should not be looked at as deviants, but as normal human beings chosing their own way of life.

All educated people should strive to change the society and its outlook through education and social awakening and action in order to raise the status of single women. The right type of education to help them to face the problems of life and build up the right attitude towards life is essential.

In this connection the media like Newspapers, Radio, TV have a large role to play in reaching the masses. Media should make deliberate attempts to negate the prejudices that exist

TABLE A.5

Problems of Single Women

Type of Problem	Spinsters				Widows				Divorced/Separated			
	Working		Non-Working		Working		Non-Working		Working		Non-Working	
	Yes	No	Yes	No	Yes	No	Yes	No	Yes	No	Yes	No
Psychological	90%	10%	94%	6%	100%	—	100%	—	100%	—	100%	—
Economic	16%	84%	100%	—	100%	—	44%	56%	76%	24%	100%	—
At Home	90%	10%	96%	4%	83%	17%	13%	77%	100%	—	100%	—
At Work	68%	32%	—	—	11%	58%	—	—	82%	18%	—	—
In Society	68%	32%	87%	13%	80%	20%	87%	13%	87%	13%	87%	13%

against singlehood. Above all there should be a sympathetic and human approach towards the problems of single women.

All single women interviewed for our study have suggested opening of 'Single Women's Homes' on the lines of 'Old Age Homes'. These institutions will help a lot of unmarried and destitute widowed and divorced women to stay in a protected environment without being a burden either to their parents or relatives. Such organisations can be run by government or voluntary organisations.

Non-working respondents who have no economic means to maintain themselves or their families, particularly children, can be provided with financial assistance. This assistance can be in the form of loans for self-employment. Again single women with some education could be enrolled in Vocational Training Institutes. The vocational training that they get must equip them with certain skills which could generate income for their subsistence. Such training will go a long way in helping financially dependent single women, not only economically but also emotionally. They will be gainfully occupied with a worthwhile activity which keeps them busy and active.

Financially a lot of widows, both working and non-working, have stressed the need for financial help and old age pension from the government, irrespective of whether their husbands were government servants or not. So also for a divorced/separated woman there is a need to provide financial assistance by way of maintenance by the government. Such assistance could be given up to the time that they are made economically independent either by giving them vocational skills or by self-employment.

Many women are not aware of the free legal aid available to them. There is a need for wide spread publicity and a campaign to make them aware of this facility. This will help a lot of women to seek legal advice on matters concerning maintenance, custody of children, etc. Above all, women in distress express extreme mental anguish and suicidal tendencies. In other words the mental health of these women was found to be extremely poor. Regular counselling by professional counsellers would help these women to ease their tensions. Individual voluntary organisations and the government could set up counselling centres where such women could come in groups or individually for help.

Divorced women have expressed discontent over delay in legal proceedings in the confirmation of separation or divorce. The concept of family courts which is recommended and already accepted should be implemented at the earliest to deal effectively with matrimonial cases.

The study of personal laws has indicated discrimination against women. Certain communities of women have less discriminatory laws than their fellow communities. In a democratic country like India where all are proclaimed equal by the Constitution of the country it seems just that in the interest of justice a uniform civil code should be introduced.

It is hoped that these suggestions will be taken seriously by the government and interested agencies concerned with the welfare of women in order to uplift the conditions of those exploited and depressed. This will not only help to alleviate the the sufferings of the single women but also enable them to lead a fuller life and thereby contribute to the development of society.

seeking divorce where such women could come in groups or individually for relief.

[illegible] women have expressed discontent [illegible] as to legal procedures in the communities of separation or divorce. The [illegible] which is [illegible] married women [illegible] at the [illegible] effective [illegible].

[illegible] has [illegible] some [illegible] [illegible] [illegible] [illegible] in the [illegible] interest of the [illegible] [illegible].

Bibliography

Books :

1. De Souza, Alfred : *Women in Contemporary India* (Ed) Traditional images and Changing roles, Indian Social Institute, Monohar, New Delhi 1975
2. Altekar, A.S. : *The position of women in Hindu Civilization from prehistoric times to the present day*, Motilal Banarisidas, Delhi 1973
3. Mehta, Sushila : *Revolution and Status of Women in India*, Metropolitian Book Co, New Delhi 1982
4. Kaur, Inderjeet : *Status of Hindu Women in India*, Chugh Publications, Allahabad 1983
5. A Synopsis of the report of the national Committee ICSSR : *Status of Women in India*, Allied Publishers Pvt Ltd New Delhi 1975
   : Status of Women in India.
6. Rani, Kala : *Role Conflict in Working Women*, Chetana Publications, New Delhi 1976
7. Jain, Devaki : *Indian Women* (Ed) Published by Director Publication Division, Ministry of Information and Broadcasting, Govt. of India, Patiala House, New Delhi 110001
8. S. Shri Devi : *A Century of Indian Womenhood*, Rao Raghavan Publisher, Prince of Wales Road, Mysore-4 1965

9. Gupta Sen, Padmini : *The Story of Women of India*, Indian Book Company, New Delhi 1974
10. Kapur, Promilla S. : *Marriage and Working Women in India*, Vikas Publishing House, New Delhi 1970
11. Report of a Seminar Organised by Central Institute of Research and Training in Public Co-operation : *Family Planning and Status of Women*, New Delhi 1972
12. Contribution of Articles on Status of Women : *Role and Status of Women in Indian Society*, Firma KLM(P) Ltd 257 B B Ganguly Street Calcutta 1978
13. Mehta, Rama : *The Western Educated Hindu Women*, Asia Publishing House New Delhi 1970
14. Nanda, B.R. ed. : *Indian Women from Purdah to Modernity*, Vikas, New Delhi 1976
15. Srivastava, Vinita : *Employment of Educated Married Women in India* National Publishing House New Delhi 1978
16. Khan, Mumtaz Ali Noor Ayesha : *Status of Rural Women in India* Uppal Publishing House New Delhi-2 1982
17. Mehta, Vimla : *Attitude of Educated Women towards Social Issues*, National Publishing House, New Delhi 1979
18. Everett, Matsajana : *Women and Social Change in India*, Heritage Publishers, New Delhi 1979
19. Blumberg, Lois Rhoda and Dwarki, Leela : *Indian Educated Women, 'Options and Constraints'*, Hindustan Publishing India Delhi 1980

20. Chatterji, Jyotsna : *The Women's decade 1975-85 : an assessment* ISPCK, Delhi for WCSRS CISRS JPW 1985

21. U. Stein, Peter : *An Overview of Singles in America*, Columbia University, New York 1958

22. Balasubramanian, A.S. : *Divorce and After*, Pub: Mrs Meena Bail No. 5, Maigunda Reva Mudaliar Road Frazer Town, Bangalore-5 1975

23. Hosier Kooiman, Helen : *The other side of Divorce*, Howthorn Books INC, New York 1975

24. Mehta, Rama : *The Divorced Hindu Women* New Delhi 1975

25. Goodie, J. William : *Women in Divorce*, Columbia University, Press New York 1956

Acts :

26. The Indian Christian Marriage Act, Bare Act (Act No 15 of 1872) : Pub: Central Law Agency, Allahabad 1984.
27. Indian Divorce Act, 1869 (Act No. 4 of 1869) : Delhi Law House, New Delhi 1984.
28. The Special Marriage Act, 1954, Marriage Amendment Laws Act (Act No 43 of 1954): Delhi Law House, Delhi.
29. Recent Changes in Laws Relating to Women : Lawyer Collective Bombay.
30. Banhi—an Occasional Journal of the Joint Women's Programme : Women and the Law Published by WCSRC, Calcutta 1981.
31. Census of India 1981 : Series I Part I I Special Report and Tables based on 5% Sample data: P. Padmanabhan.

20. Chhetri, Leela ... *The Women's Academy* [illegible]
ISPCK, Delhi [illegible]
CISRS [illegible]

21. [illegible] Stuart, Peter ... *An Outline of* [illegible]
Anglican Communion [illegible]
New York, 1958.

Mecca Law [illegible]
Reva, Modaliar Road, Cantonment
Town, Bangalore-5 1975.

New Horizon Books [illegible]
New York, 1975.

New Delhi 1975.

1956.

OUR OUTSTANDING PUBLICATIONS

Author	Title	Price
Ahangar, Mohd. Altaf Hussain	Customary Succession Among Muslims.	175.00
Amir Hussain, IAS	A Trinbe in Turmoil : Socio-Economic Study of Jammu Gujars of Uttar Pradesh	150.00
Balasubamanian, M.	Nehru : A Study in Secularism.	45.00
Banerjee, Pramathanath	Public Administration in Ancient India.	125.00
Barman, Kiran	Public Debt Management in India.	150.00
Baruah, A.K.	Systems Analysis in Political Science : A Marxit Critique of David Easton.	125.00
Bawa, Noorjahan	People's Participation Development Adm. in India	125.00
Bayti, Jamnalal	Readings in Education.	150.00
Bayti, Jamnalal	Problems of Education in the third world.	150.00
Bhattacharjee, Debasish	Bureacracy and Development in Meghalaya.	150.00
Bhattacharya, Mohit	Management of Urban Government in India	50.00
Bhattacharya, Mohit	Bureaucracy and development Administration.	50.00
Bhargava, P.K.	Essays on Indian Economic Planning.	90.00
Bhargava, P.K.	Some Aspects of Indian Public Finances.	125.00
Bijan Mohanta	Administrative Development of Arunachal Pradesh, 1875-1975.	150.00
Biswas, Atreyi	Political, Social and Cultural History of Ancient India (H).	125.00
Centre for Policy Research, N. Delhi	Population, Poverty and Hope.	300.00
Chaudhari, R.L.	The Concept of Secularism in Indian Constitution	200.00
Desmukh, C.D.	Amarakosa : Gems from the Treasure House of Sanskrit Words.	90.00
Dey, Bata K.	Bureaucracy Development and Public Management in India.	80.00
Durrany, K.S.	Religion in Society.	200.00

Author	Title	Price
Gabriel, Soloman	Foreign policy of Canada	125.00
Ghosh, Partha S.	Sino-Soviet Relations : U.S. Perception and Policy Resp.	100.00
Ghosh, Shubhra	Female Criminals in India.	125.00
Handa, K.L.	Programme Performance Budgeting.	75.00
Jagannadham, V.	Administration and Social Change.	60.00
Jain, Anil Kumar	Some Aspects of Income-Tax Administration in India.	100.00
Jain, D.K.	Project Planning and Appraisal in Planned Economy : The India Context.	75.00
Jain, R.B. and P.N. Chaudhuri	Bureaucratic Values in Development.	120.00
Jain, R.B.	Comparative Legislative Behaviour.	50.00
Kaushik, S.N.	Pakistan under Bhutto's Leadership.	175.00
Kamble, N.D.	Bonded Labour in India.	60.00
Kamble, N.D.	Migrants in Indian Metropolis.	75.00
Kedia, Kusum Lata	Local Finance in an Indian State : Municipal Finance of Varanasi Division Since 1951	200.00
Khan, Mumtaz Ali	Scheduled Caste and their Status in India.	75.00
Khan, Mumtaz Ali	Status of Rural Women in India.	75.00
Khan, Mumtaz Ali	Social Legislation and the Rural Poor.	50.00
Khan, Mumtaz Ali	Muslims in the Process of Rural Development in India.	150.00
Mandal, B.B.	Tribals at the Polls : A Study of Khunti in Chotanagpur.	90.00
Madan, J.C.	Indian Police.	110.00
Mahendra Singh	Indo-U.S. Relations : A Political Study.	75.00
Malik, Inder Lal	Dalai Lamas of Tibet	90.00
Menon, M. Indu	Status of Muslim Women in India.	50.00
Mishra, Upendra	Caste and Politics in India.	225.00
Mishra, S.N. and Kushal Sharma	Problems and Prospects of Rural Development in India.	80.00
Mohan, N. Shantha	Status of Nurses in India.	60.00

Mukarji, Nirmal and Ashis Banerjee	Democracy Federalism and the future of Indias Unity.	60.00
Pal, J.J.	Jinnah and the creation of Pakistan.	75.00
Paliwal, M.R.	Social Change and Education.	175.00
Paliwai, M.R.	The Teacher Education on the Move : Today and Tomorrow.	225.00
Paliwal. M.R.	Differential Effectiveness of Micro-learning.	50.00
Pai Panandiker, V.A. and Arun Sud.	Changing Political Representation in India.	65.00
Pai Panandiker, V.A. and Ajay K. Mehta	People's Participation in Family Planning.	160.00
Pai Panandiker, V.A. R N. Bisnnoi and O.P. Sharma	Organisational Policy for Family Planning.	125.00
Pai Panandiker, V.A. and P.N. Chaudhuri	Demographic Transition in Goa and its Policy Implications.	40.00
Panda, Basudev	Indian Bureaucracy : An Inside Story.	60.00
Pandey, K.K.	Rural Development in India : Continuity and Change.	125.00
Pandey, Jawaharlal	State Politics in India.	90.00
Partap Singh	Urban Government in India.	45.00
Pillai, G. Narayana	Social Background of Policy Leadership in India.	90.00
Rai, Haridwar and S.P. Singh	Current Ideas and Issues in Indian Administration.	70.00
Rajgopal, P.R.	Communal Violence in India.	140.00
Rajjan Lal and Kidwai, Nasira	Practical Cataloguing Procedure (Hindi).	95.00
Rastogi, P.N.	India 1981-86 : A forecaste on Economic, Political and Social Developments.	50.00
Reddy, P. Ranjani	The Role of Dominant Caste in Indian Politics.	150.00
Rawlinson, H.G.	Shivaji the Maratha : his Life and Time.	75.00
Ray, B. Datta	The Emergence and Role of Middle Class in North East India.	100.00

Ray, B. Datta	The Pattern and Problems of Population in North-East India.	250.00
Rita Khanna	Agricultural Mechanisation and Social Change in India.	125.00
Roy, R.C., IAS	State Public Enterprise in India.	200.00
Saksena, H.S.	Safeguards for Scheduled Castes and Tribes : Founding Father's View.	200.00
Seshadri, K.	Studies in the problems of the third world.	175.00
Seshadri, K.	Studies in Indian Polity.	150.00
Sharma, P.D.	Police and Criminal Justice Administration in India.	125.00
Sharma, P.D.	Police, Polity and People in India.	125.00
Sharma, R.N. & Bakshi Santosh	Tribes and Tribal Development : Select Bibliography.	250.00
Sharma, T.R.	New Challenges in Indian Politics.	175.00
Shrivastava, M.P.	Problems of Accountability of Public Enterprises in India.	225.00
Sikka, R.P.	The Civil Service in India.	150.00
Sinha, R.P.	Social Dimensions of Trade Unionism in India.	90.00
Singh, L.P.	Electoral Reform.	95.00
Singh, L.P.	India's Foreign Policy.	55.00
Singh, S.P.	Perspectives in Indian Politics and Administration.	60.00
Singh, S.S.	Administration of Natural Justice in India.	250.00
Singh, S.S. and S. Sundram	Emerging Harijan Elite : A Study of their Identity.	125.00
Sundeep Khanna, IAS	Civil Administration in India.	60.00
Trivedi, B.V.	Prison Administration in India : Model Prison Programme.	175.00
Verma, S.P.	Indian Parliamentarians: A Study of the Socio-Political Background.	90.00
Vijay Kumar	India and Srilanka-China Relations 1948-84.	125.00
Wishwakarama, R.K.	Urban and Regional Planning Policy in India.	75.00